D1647289

Critical Guides to German Texts

5 Stifter: Bunte Steine

Critical Guides to German Texts

EDITED BY MARTIN SWALES

STIFTER

Bunte Steine

Eve Mason

Fellow of Newnham College, Cambridge

Grant & Cutler Ltd
1986

72063

© Grant & Cutler Ltd
1986

Library of Congress Cataloging-in-Publication Data

Mason, Eve, 1921-
  Stifter, Bunte Steine

  (Critical guides to German texts; 5)
  Bibliography: p.
  Includes index.
  1. Stifter, Adalbert, 1805-1868. Bunte Steine.
I. Title.   II. Series.
PT2525.B863M37 1986   833'.7   86-82407
ISBN 0-7293-0246-6

I.S.B.N. 84-599-1869-6

DEPÓSITO LEGAL: V. 97 - 1987

Printed in Spain by
Artes Gráficas Soler, S.A., Valencia
for
GRANT & CUTLER LTD
55-57, GREAT MARLBOROUGH STREET, LONDON W1V 2AY
and
27, SOUTH MAIN STREET, WOLFEBORO, NH 03894-2069, USA

Contents

Prefatory Note

The edition of *Bunte Steine* referred to in this study is the Goldmann paperback edition. I refer to it by page number following the quotations. Full details of this and of the standard editions of Stifter's works are listed in the Select Bibliography. References to the early versions of the stories are to the Historisch-kritische Gesamtausgabe, edited by Alfred Doppler and Wolfgang Frühwald, 1978-, as given in the Bibliography. The abbreviation used is Jf. (Journalfassung), followed by page number. References to Stifter's letters and to his other writings are to the 1901-1979 standard edition, edited by August Sauer and others; abbreviation: SW, followed by the number of the volume in Roman numerals and the page number.

The figures in parentheses in italic type refer to numbered items in the Select Bibliography; the italic figure is usually followed by a page reference. Among the many general studies which deal with the life and writings of Adalbert Stifter I recommend a selection which I hope will give the reader a useful start. Because there is no convenient monograph on the *Bunte Steine* collection, I have listed a number of essays and articles on the various tales. In this list there are several items which I have inserted to provide the reader with views different from and opposed to mine.

I should like here to thank Professor Martin Swales for including me in this series of Critical Guides, and my husband for advice on matters of English idiom.

1. 'Vorrede'

In his *Life of Goethe* (the first to be written in English) George Henry Lewes wrote the following about German criticism devoted to *Wilhelm Meister*:

No one acquainted with Germany or German literature can fail to recognize the widespread and pernicious influence of a mistaken application of Philosophy to Art: an application which becomes a tyranny on the part of the real thinker, and a hideous absurdity on the part of those who merely echo the jargon of the schools. It is this criticism which has stifled art in Germany and ruined many a young artist who showed promise. It is a fundamental mistake to translate Art into the formulas of Philosophy, and then christen the translation the Philosophy of Art. The critic is never easy until he has shifted his ground. He is not content with the work as it presents itself. He endeavours to get behind it, beneath it, into the depths of the soul that produced it. He is not satisfied with what the artist has *given*, he wants to know what he *meant* ... Thus the phantom of Philosophy hovers mistily before Art, concealing Art from our eyes.[1]

What Lewes wrote in 1864 is largely true of German literary critics today, and particularly of those who in recent years have written articles or books on Stifter and his literary works. Goethe, who was well aware of this tendency on the part of Germans to look for an idea in a work of art, laughed at and rejected it as a mode of treating literature. Eckermann reports a vigorous outburst made on 6 May 1827:

[1] George Henry Lewes, *Life of Goethe* (London, Routledge, 1864), p.397.

Die Deutschen sind übrigens wunderliche Leute! — Sie machen sich durch ihre tiefen Gedanken und Ideen, die sie überall suchen und überall hineinlegen, das Leben schwerer als billig. — Ei! So habt doch endlich einmal die Courage, euch den Eindrücken hinzugeben, euch ergötzen zu lassen, euch rühren zu lassen, euch erheben zu lassen, ja euch belehren und zu etwas Großem entflammen und ermutigen zu lassen; aber denkt nur nicht immer, es wäre alles eitel, wenn es nicht irgend abstrakter Gedanke und Idee wäre![2]

Stifter, however, appears to have welcomed these 'phantoms of Philosophy' and to have belittled the appeal made by Goethe to let the work of art make its own impact on the reader. In a letter to a friend he appears in the guise of a man with a philosophical mission, a purveyor of abstract, would-be lofty, moral ideas. He writes that he has never made any claim to be a great writer or to be esteemed for his imaginative gift. Such a person, he states, would be a high priest of humanity and such an ideal is too high for him. What he has tried to do in his writings is to provide good people with good reading, to share with them feelings and views he regards as worthy and of high value. And he continues:

das Reich des Reinen Einfachen Schönen, das nicht nur häufig aus der Litteratur sondern auch aus dem Leben zu verschwinden droht, auszubreiten und in einer nicht ganz unschönen Gestalt vor die Leser zu treten, das war und ist das Streben meiner Schriften. (23 March 1852)[3]

When we hear Stifter making so much of 'das Reich des Reinen Einfachen Schönen', we might be pardoned for thinking he had in mind something similar to Winckelmann's 'edle Einfalt, stille Größe', a phrase with which he described the

[2] Johann Wolfgang Goethe, *Gedenkausgabe der Werke, Briefe und Gespräche*, edited by Ernst Beutler, 24 volumes (Zürich, Artemis, 1948-1964), XXIV, p.635.

[3] All references to Stifter's letters are to SW, XVII, XVIII, XIX, by date of letter.

impression made on him by Greek art and formulated its essence. But Stifter was clearly using his terms to build up, not a cool description, but what is virtually a wishful dream of a moral mission to humanity. It was while he was a pupil in the monastery school of Kremsmünster that Stifter first met with the idea, which goes back to scholastic philosophy and was reinforced by the teaching of Leibniz and Wolff, that the beautiful is nothing but the divine, dressed in a graceful garment. The divine, however, he was taught, is manifested in man only to a limited extent, but in God, completely. Nevertheless it was regarded as an essential part of human nature, as a power everywhere striving to reveal itself as the good, the true, and the beautiful in religion, in learning, in art and in conduct. Much later, Stifter confessed that this thought, which had struck him so forcibly as a boy, in the very centre of his being, had remained with him all his life: it had, he tells us, been confirmed by all his later experiences during his twenty-two years in Vienna, by all his attempts to acquire learning and to write stories and by all his human contacts in his official duties as an inspector of schools. The main principle underlying his writing, he says, had always been to be human on the human level, to love the highest when he saw it, to rejoice in God's creation. He had never felt too lofty to handle earthly concerns and to devote himself to the business of life. Yet at the same time he had always been willing to sacrifice himself for higher things and to keep in constant invisible communion with the aspirations of those who led a spiritual life.

If the claim to be a philosopher is to be sustained for Stifter, it is not enough to trace the abstract words he uses back to their original contexts in Plato or the New Testament. Stifter must be shown not only to have taken over the names for these things, but also to have dealt with the substances these words point to. Otherwise his apparent juggling with them will be nothing more than what has been styled a dance of bloodless categories. He will be open to the charge of having tried to manufacture their substance by, as it were, spinning them out of his own bowels, of having, as Yeats put it, made 'lock, stock and barrel out of his bitter soul'.

Far be it from me to doubt Stifter's sincerity when he is protesting his missionary zeal. Indeed, I think that, up to a point,
we ought to regard it as his main source of inspiration and the
creative impulse behind his characteristic mode of writing. But
there is a difference between a deeply felt personal belief in
certain important values in life and the kind of seeking after
knowledge which deals with ultimate reality, the most general
causes and principles of things and ideas, that we usually
associate with the term 'philosophy' and which would allow us
to speak of Stifter in the same breath with which we call Kant,
Hegel or Schopenhauer great German philosophers.

The principal claim made for Stifter as a philosopher concerns
what he expounds in the *Vorrede* to *Bunte Steine* under the
heading of 'sanftes Gesetz', as we find it, for instance in this
sentence: 'Wir wollen das sanfte Gesetz zu erblicken suchen,
wodurch das menschliche Geschlecht geleitet wird' (p.9). Open
any German literary history and you will find Stifter described
as 'der Dichter des sanften Gesetzes'. The concept of the 'sanfte
Gesetz' has been allowed to intrude everywhere, even where
Stifter's intentions do not warrant it. It has been seen as a
panacea for all discord, a magic spell which harmonises, by
spiriting them away, all differences and difficulties, even where,
as so often, Stifter's works tell a quite different tale.

The odd thing is that nobody has been quite sure what the
'sanfte Gesetz' really is and how it works, if we judge by the
disparity of interpretations offered. While some critics, stressing
the important debt to eighteenth-century thought in his central
concepts of 'Vernunft' and 'Humanität', have hailed Stifter as
an upholder of tradition (*9*), others have seen the formulation of
the 'sanfte Gesetz' as a reflection of a modern, empirical
approach to science (*3*); still others have seen in it an expression
of Stifter's awareness of the relentless development of bourgeois
society (*5*).

Stifter must undoubtedly take some of the blame for this
uncertainty of critical interpretation. On the one hand, it was
always part of his didactic aim to prompt the reader to active
participation by forcing him to find the author's meaning by
reading between the lines rather than to await explicit

explanation. On the other hand, and this applies particularly to this *Vorrede*, some blame attaches to him if it turns out to be a fact that his failure to argue logically springs from an inner contradiction; if his contentions have their origins in intuitive hopes, longings and anxieties rather than in cool observation of the facts of life.

The opening of the *Vorrede* makes an immediate impact on the reader. The first page is a concentrated credo — the author's passionate claim in his small way to be doing something great. He reiterates his view that for him art is 'nach der Religion das Höchste auf Erden' (p.7), and that his own aim as a writer is 'ein Körnlein Gutes zu dem Baue des Ewigen beizutragen' (p.7). Although he thrice pronounces 'ich halte' ('I hold it for true that'), he buttresses this personal affirmation with what look on the surface like general observations resembling those made by natural scientists. Indeed, he rests his whole case (i.e. that he is about his Father's business by giving close attention to the less striking aspects of human life in his stories) on an analogy with the procedure of scientists searching for the most general laws governing the workings of the universe.

In order to make the case for his own estimate of the truly great plausible, and at the same time to support his view that everyday life is 'greater' than the mighty deeds we read of in epics or the emotional upheavals in great tragedies, he has to persuade us that the scientist too does not regard the great convulsions which shake the heavens, the earth and the oceans as 'important' in comparison with humdrum observations such as the recordings of the boiling point of milk on a stove. Secondly, he has to persuade us that the scientist does *not* formulate large-scale hypotheses about the nature of matter which he tries to prove or disprove in a series of experiments, but *is* restricted to the crudest inductive procedure in which he gropes his way like a mole or accumulates trivial data like an ant. But above all, Stifter's greatest leap is the assertion that there is an analogy between the study of matter and the study of the moral and spiritual universe.

In this *Vorrede*, of course, Stifter is not laying all his cards on the table, nor is he performing a scientific demonstration.

Rather is he trying to 'bounce' us into accepting enough of this analogy to render his personal claim as a writer more acceptable. Now, while we might be willing to accept without further ado that the attitude of the natural scientist resembles in some ways that of the moralist, at least in the sense that both investigators are accumulating 'data' and attempting to find connections between their data which might eventually produce 'laws', we need far more than anything given by Stifter in this *Vorrede* before we can believe that matter behaves according to laws such as those we discover when investigating the moral patterns of human behaviour. Stifter does nothing to justify the 'scientific' sense of 'Gesetz' when applied to morals, and still less to make it clear that the laws matter observes resemble the laws which impose themselves on our moral sense. Those who regard Stifter as a Moses bringing us a new commandment with his 'sanfte Gesetz' are therefore, in my opinion, taking the will for the deed.

The reader who notes the confident tone of the whole *Vorrede* and in particular the claim that the views being put forward differ from the fashionable may be surprised to learn that the two leading thoughts, that of the analogy between the physical and the moral world and the likeness of the dominating force in both, are by no means original. For it is clear that by one route or another these two ideas reached Stifter by way of Herder. Nevertheless it is not true that this preface is a mere summary of *Ideen zur Philosophie der Geschichte der Menschheit* or, as has been recently suggested (6, p.32) that Stifter's 'sanftes Gesetz' is a condensed version of Herder's Book 15 of the *Ideen*. Although Herder generally makes much of the term 'Humanität', and at several points in this particular book seems to be identifying the laws of physics and those of morals, as here:

Ist indessen ein Gott in der Natur: so ist er auch in der Geschichte: denn auch der Mensch ist ein Theil der Schöpfung und muß in seinen wildesten Ausschweifungen und Leidenschaften Gesetze befolgen, die nicht minder schön und vortreflich sind, als jene, nach welchen sich alle

Himmels- und Erdkörper bewegen (SW, XIV, p.207).[4]

a close comparison of both texts reveals essential differences.

In the theory of philosophy Herder comes after the rationalism of Leibniz and his followers and looks forward to the relativism and positivism of the nineteenth century. His idea of an analogy between the physical and moral worlds is based on the pantheistic doctrine that God is everything and everything is God. He defines God in terms of 'Kraft': 'Gott erfüllt den Raum durch seine Kraft' (SW, XXXII, p.228). His pantheism enables him to overcome all opposition between God and nature, and to assimilate the divine 'Kraft' to the 'organische Kräfte' or nature. He can therefore cheerfully allow his scientists to trace the dynamic power in and behind the phenomena of nature and the many particular 'Kräfte' into which the universal 'Kraft' differentiates itself while God 'der oberste Haushalter siehet und hält die Kette aller auf einander dringenden Kräfte' (SW, XIII, p.169).

Nowhere in Stifter's *Vorrede* do we find such a specific definition of the concept of 'Kraft' nor of its divine origin. If Herder can at times be accused of vagueness and contradictions in his usage of the term, Stifter's adaptation is even more indeterminate. It should be obvious that if we take away this belief in the relation of God and nature, all the technical terms, and above all, 'Kraft', used by Herder must suffer a sea change in the mouth of Stifter. But the most radical difference between them comes out in their divergent treatment of the violent, uncontrollable outbursts of passion, such as those which figure so largely in Homer's *Iliad* or any of the greater Greek tragedies.

Herder considered that the human race owes its development and particularly the sharpening of its intelligence to these very same all-destructive elemental passions and he thought that these passions contributed to the general good just as storms at sea are parts of a harmonious cosmic order:

[4] Johann Gottfried Herder, *Sämmtliche Werke*, edited by B. Suphan, 33 volumes (Berlin, 1877-1933). All references are to this edition (abbreviated SW) by volume and page following the quotation.

Nicht anders ists mit den wütenden Leidenschaften der
Menschen, diesen Stürmen auf dem Meer, diesem ver-
wüstenden Feuerelemente. Eben durch sie und an ihnen
hat unser Geschlecht seine Vernunft geschärft und tausend
Mittel, Regeln und Künste erfunden, sie nicht nur einzu-
schränken, sondern selbst zum Besten zu lenken, wie die
ganze Geschichte zeiget. Ein Leidenschaftsloses Menschen-
geschlecht hätte auch seine Vernunft nie ausgebildet; es
läge noch irgend in einer Troglodytenhöle (SW, XIV,
p.221.)

And again:

Alle Irrthümer des Menschen sind ein Nebel der Wahrheit;
alle Leidenschaften seiner Brust sind wildere Triebe einer
Kraft, die sich selbst noch nicht kennet, die ihrer Natur
nach aber nicht anders als aufs Bessere wirket. Auch die
Stürme des Meers, oft zertrümmernd und verwüstend, sind
Kinder einer harmonischen Weltordnung und müssen der-
selben wie die säuselnden Zephyrs dienen (SW, XIV,
p.215).

What a contrast, we might feel, between this joyous affirmation
and Stifter's cautious, even grudging, account: 'Es gibt Kräfte,
die nach dem Bestehen des Einzelnen zielen', (p.9) and his state-
ment that the fiercer passions are 'so gut Hervorbringungen
einzelner und einseitiger Kräfte ... wie Stürme, feuerspeiende
Berge, Erdbeben.' (p.9). When we find Stifter neglecting to
provide any rational arguments to support and clarify these
assertions, may we not suspect that they issue from a deep and
almost irrational fear of the destructive forces in man and
nature?

Stifter's own conception of the moral law, we might also feel,
is a lesser thing and on a more confined scale than Herder's.

Wenn aber jemand jedes Ding unbedingt an sich reißt, was
sein Wesen braucht, wenn er die Bedingungen des Daseins
eines anderen zerstört, so ergrimmt etwas Höheres in uns,

wir helfen dem Schwachen und Unterdrückten, wir stellen
den Stand wieder her, daß er ein Mensch neben dem
andern bestehe und seine menschliche Bahn gehen könne,
und wenn wir das getan haben, so fühlen wir uns ... als
ganze Menschheit (p.9f.).

Although Stifter never makes clear what he meant by 'etwas
Höheres', it is plain enough that this account points to the
existence of an innate moral sense.

These are not the observations of an innovator in moral philosophy. Stifter is not, as has been stated, in this sense a
'Gesetzgeber' (*9*, p.81). But all his moral reflections are evidence
of his deep feeling for the essential constituents of a peaceful
and useful community. They exhibit a sense of justice, a relish
for simplicity of conduct, self-mastery, and obedience to the
laws of reason. The rational grounds for his condemnation of
the destructive element in society, as we see from the quotation
given above, are connected with his perception of the damage
done to the possibilities of life for the other members of the
community, and even here, Stifter seems to be positing an
incidental good arising from society's reaction against such
violence. But this simple outline of a morally blameless life does
not constitute a philosophy. It is by a leap of feeling that the
parallel is drawn with 'das Wehen der Luft, das Rieseln des
Wassers, das Wachsen der Getreide, das Wogen des Meeres, das
Grünen der Erde, das Glänzen des Himmels, das Schimmern der
Gestirne' (p.7) — the phenomena which he regards as great and
important features of Nature. But by elevating these 'constants'
of natural processes into 'das Allgemeine' and 'allein Welter-
haltende' (p.8), Stifter is implicitly dismissing the fearful aspects
of nature which Kant thought gave rise in us to the sense of the
sublime: 'Aber ihr Anblick wird nur um desto anziehender, je
furchtbarer er ist, wenn wir uns nur in Sicherheit befinden; und
wir nennen diese Gegenstände gern erhaben, weil sie die Seelen-
stärke über ihr gewöhnliches Mittelmaß erhöhen, und ein
Vermögen zu widerstehen von ganz anderer Art in uns
entdecken lassen, welches uns Mut macht, uns mit der schein-

baren Allgewalt der Natur messen zu können.'[5]

It is strange, however, that Stifter's elevation to the status of 'groß' of these regularly recurring phenomena of nature did not bring with it such belief in the cyclical interpretation of human history as we find occupying a prominent place in Herder's writings. There is indeed one such gesture in this direction, but it comes as near to charlatanism as anything in the *Vorrede*. It is the claim that there is a parallel with the various accounts given down the ages of what are the great features of nature and the rise and the fall of civilisations when morality decays. 'Wie in der Geschichte der Natur die Ansichten über das Große sich stets geändert haben, so ist es auch in der sittlichen Geschichte der Menschen gewesen' (p.11). Nobody, as far as I know, has been able to give a meaning to this 'wie ... so', or to describe any such process of development, flowering and decay or any laws whatever governing the changing attitudes towards nature in the history of man's thinking. It is here that we may detect an element of special pleading in the *Vorrede*, which emerges into daylight when the petty, though decent, activities of men, constantly repeated down the ages, are likened to a silver stream, while the turbulent upheavals which make human history terrible and tragic, horrible and glorious, are swept under the carpet. The exaggeration here forces the reader to protest that the babbling of the silver stream is nothing more than the chronicling of small beer, and that life would have no dignity and grandeur if Stifter's predilections were taken to represent the main line of human history. But the whole tone of the *Vorrede* protects Stifter from any imputation of a conscious will to mislead. Although the records are too scanty to enable us to reconstruct the inner workings of Stifter's mind during these years, the personal details available to us allow us to conjecture that this empty argument was an attempt to cover up problems which caused him deep anxiety when he came to find them insoluble.

[5] Immanuel Kant, *Studienausgabe*, edited by Wilhelm Weischedel, 6 volumes (Darmstadt, Wissenschaftliche Buchgesellschaft, 1975), V, *Kritik der Urteilskraft*, § 28, p.349. Cf. for a similar view, Herbert Seidler, *Österreichischer Vormärz und Goethezeit* (Wien, Österreichische Akademie der Wissenschaften, 1982), pp.381-89.

This anxiety comes to the fore in the vivid account of the decline of civilisation from a decent moral standard. It is impossible not to believe that here he has his own world in mind, and that therefore he is calling into question the very validity of the 'sanfte Gesetz', which should have rendered this decline impossible. The aridity of the style in this passage seems to indicate that black despair had gripped Stifter, for the passage is one long catalogue of human failings culminating in a spectral vision of the untrammelled expansion of the ego resulting in the total surrender of the civilisation either to internal strife or the outer enemy:

> Untergehenden Völkern verschwindet zuerst das Maß. Sie gehen nach Einzelnem aus, sie werfen sich mit kurzem Blick auf das Beschränkte und Unbedeutende, sie setzen das Bedingte über das Allgemeine; dann suchen sie den Genuß und das Sinnliche, sie suchen Befriedigung ihres Hasses und Neides gegen den Nachbar, in ihrer Kunst wird das Einseitige geschildert, das nur von einem Standpunkte Gültige, dann das Zerfahrene, Umstimmende, Abenteuerliche, endlich das Sinnenreizende, und zuletzt die Unsitte und das Laster, in der Religion sinkt das Innere zur bloßen Gestalt oder zur üppigen Schwärmerei herab, der Unterschied zwischen Gut und Böse verliert sich, der einzelne verachtet das Ganze und geht seiner Lust und seinem Verderben nach, und so wird das Volk eine Beute seiner inneren Zerwirrung oder die eines äußeren, wilderen, aber kräftigeren Feindes (p.12).

The explanation for this loss of faith in the 'sanfte Gesetz' is to be sought in the remark with which Stifter rounds off the *Vorrede*:

> ... meine eben entwickelten Ansichten und die Erlebnisse der letztvergangenen Jahre lehrten mich, meiner Kraft zu mißtrauen ... (p.12).

There can be little doubt that this last paragraph expresses

Stifter's abhorrence of the events during and after the abortive
revolution of 1848. Whereas Goethe, despite his deep dislike of
the cruelties of the French Revolution, could still say in 1792
that the sublimity of the event swallowed the particular misery
of the French Revolution, and on 14 March 1830 calmly state to
Eckermann: 'Bei keiner Revolution sind die Extreme zu
vermeiden. Bei der politischen will man anfänglich gewöhnlich
nichts weiter als die Abstellung von allerlei Mißbräuchen; aber
ehe man es sich versieht, steckt man tief in Blutvergießen und
Greueln',[6] Stifter's reaction to the events of 1848 betrays a deep
personal fear that, successful or unsuccessful, the Revolution
was going to unleash 'nicht meßbare Gewalten' which would
ultimately destroy reason and humanity (letter of 25 May 1848).
It was a final shattering of his legacy from the eighteenth
century, the belief that men are rational, decent people
influenced by truth and objective standards, who can be safely
released from the outward restraints of convention and
traditional standards and inflexible rules of conduct, and left to
their own sensible devices, pure motives and reliable intuitions
of the good. In March 1849 he maintained that the ideal of
freedom had been destroyed for years to come. The man who
was morally free, he said, may be free politically, indeed he
always was, but if he was not morally free, no power on earth
could make him so, and added: 'Es gibt nur eine Macht, die es
kann: *Bildung*' (6 March 1849). The several articles he wrote to
make the people aware of their new duties as an electorate end in
an emotional cry for the need for men who knew their own
minds and were of sterling integrity. But where were such people
to be found?

For these reasons I would abandon the search for deep philosophical thought in this *Vorrede* in favour of a different
approach. For it may very well be that a more probable
explanation is to be found in Stifter's attempt to come to terms
with his times. The year is 1852. He had already written on 21
November 1848: 'Möge Vernunft und Menschlichkeit siegen —
zwei Dinge, die jetzt fast aus der Welt geflohen zu sein

---

[6] Johann Wolfgang Goethe, *Gedenkausgabe der Werke, Briefe und Gespräche*,
edited by Ernst Beutler, 24 volumes (Zürich, Artemis, 1948-1964), XXIV, p.726.

scheinen.' In his distress he turned to nature and its inherent laws to provide a formula which would ensure the continuity he so fervently wished for in the political arena. He had had an especially vivid relation to nature ever since his childhood years in the small village of Oberplan. This interest was strengthened by his study of the natural sciences. But his attitude to nature is not that of the scientist content to observe and note all its aspects. His use of what he calls natural laws is dictated by an almost mystical fervour to find parallels in the natural and the moral spheres which would allow him to formulate his elusive conception of an all-embracing law, and give it some substance and standing.

In one of his letters he describes how he used to lie awake at night worrying over the political situation and deeply conscious of his inexperience and ineptitude in dealing with political matters. His predicament was that of many well-meaning Austrian liberals who hoped for peaceful reform and were keenly aware that violent revolution would spell the end of the multi-national Habsburg empire. Although, as will become abundantly apparent from an examination of the stories in *Bunte Steine*, Stifter had a particular fear, an almost irrational fear of any violent passion, which arose from his own passionate and divided self, his concept of the 'sanfte Gesetz' was generated from a deeper concern for human values than his personal predicament. What he hoped was that the values of human conduct which had proved capable of maintaining life and civilisation in the past could be ensured to continue in a society in imminent danger of breaking up. It is greatly to his credit that he claimed and supported the rights of everybody without distinction, 'das Gesetz der Gerechtigkeit, das Gesetz der Sitte, das Gesetz, das will, daß jeder geachtet, geehrt, ungefährdet neben dem anderen bestehe, daß er seine höhere menschliche Laufbahn gehen könne...' (p.10). Yet so ghostly and immaterial is his law of the 'sanfte Gesetz' that it could not engage with the real forces with which Austria was involved, the conflict of unyielding claims, the authority of the state, the authority of the church, the authority of the absolute monarchy, and the authority of the people. Amid all this violent conflict, one can understand how

Stifter came to turn away with a shudder from all forms of violence in nature and in the soul.

The reflections in the *Vorrede* constitute more than a personal document thanks to the style they are written in. His didactic impulse is clear, but his fascinating, evocative prose manages to carry it off and, at times, to express considerable subtleties of thought. Stifter always maintained that art is the capacity to bring into being that which grips the heart by its extraordinary beauty, raises us up, makes us finer, softens us so that we become capable of good actions, and, finally, prepares us to enter into reverent contact with and worship of God. Again he said, art is not what one makes but the way in which one makes it. These thoughts are exemplified in this preface. It is an audacity of style and structure which lifts our thoughts above the private and ordinary level. It is a sheer expressiveness of language which almost makes us believe that he has bridged the vast gaps in the logic of the argument. What persuades us is an incantatory quality in the repetitions and parallels of phrases. There is, for instance, an imaginative felicity of touch in the use of verbal nouns in the sentence quoted earlier, 'das Wehen der Luft' etc., which works every time it is read over. The phrases force us first to see and then to experience the active thriving in all living things. There is a similar felicity in bringing together two such disparate things as 'sanft' and 'Gesetz'. The weary war-torn spirit is lulled by the soothing lilt of 'daß er als Kleinod gehütet werde, wie jeder Mensch ein Kleinod für alle andern Menschen ist' (p.10). The fourfold use of the same conjunctions 'so ... wie' introducing and uniting the sweeping analogies intended to reconcile disparate spheres itself goes some way towards persuading us that a pervading harmony has been set up, and to that extent would account for the popular description of Stifter as 'der Dichter des sanften Gesetzes'.

Yet the persuasive beauty of the prose style cannot totally blind us to the vacuity of some of the more rhetorical passages of the *Vorrede* or the excessive degree of abstraction of some of the key formulations, which therefore cannot hold the spectre of national decline at bay for any length of time. It is in his narrative prose that Stifter emerges as a true artist, and oddly enough as a greater mind and a greater personality than in his theoretical reflections. He is much closer in his stories to the actual pulse of life, and less afraid to face the problems posed by the more violent passions and the grandiose spectacle of elemental natural forces.

2. 'Granit'

On a first reading *Granit* might well be taken for a simple tale about country folk. A small boy is punished by his mother for a harmless prank. His grandfather comforts him by taking him on an errand to a neighbouring village, and on the way talks to him about the valley in which they live and tells him something of its history. They return in the evening to a world of peace:

> Als wir durch das Vorhaus gingen, wo ich in solche Strafe gekommen war, zwitscherten die jungen Schwalben leise in ihrem Neste wie schlaftrunken, in der großen Stube brannte ein Lämpchen auf dem Tische, das alle Samstagnächte die ganze Nacht zu Ehren der heiligen Jungfrau brannte, in dem Schlafgemach der Eltern lag der Vater in dem Bette, hatte ein Licht neben sich und las, wie er gewöhnlich zu tun pflegte ... (p.45).

But on closer inspection it becomes apparent that this is no artless tale, but on the contrary has been shaped in every detail by a conscious, artistic purpose. There is deliberate artifice in giving the central incident a framework. The first-person narrator is a grown man, who recalls an incident from his childhood. Stifter in fact seems to have drawn on an incident in his own childhood which closely tallies with the story of the small boy's terror when he finds he has aroused such unwonted displeasure in his mother and received such disproportionate punishment.

> Ich fand mich einmal wieder in dem Entsezlichen, Zugrunderichtenden von dem ich ... gesagt habe. Dann war Klingen, Verwirrung, Schmerz in meinen Händen und Blut daran, die Mutter verband mich, und dann war ein Bild, das so klar vor mir jezt dasteht, als wäre es in

reinlichen Farben auf Porzellan gemalt. Ich stand in dem Garten, der von damals zuerst in meiner Einbildungskraft ist, die Mutter war da, dann die andere Großmutter, deren Gestalt in jenem Augenblike auch zum ersten Male in mein Gedächtniß kam, in mir war die Erleichterung, die alle Male auf das Weichen des Entsezlichen und Zugrunderichtenden folgte, und ich sagte: 'Mutter, da wächst ein Kornhalm'. Die Großmutter antwortete darauf: 'Mit einem Knaben, der die Fenster zerschlagen hat, redet man nicht.' Ich verstand zwar den Zusammenhang nicht, aber das Außerordentliche, das eben von mir gewichen war, kam sogleich wieder, die Mutter sprach wirklich kein Wort, und ich erinnere mich, daß ein ganz Ungeheures auf meiner Seele lag.[7]

In *Granit* this deeply disturbing experience is expressed in a beautifully economical but highly expressive sentence:

Ich war, obwohl es mir schon von Anfange bei der Sache immer nicht so ganz vollkommen geheuer gewesen war, doch über diese fürchterliche Wendung der Dinge, und weil ich mit meiner teuersten Verwandten auf dieser Erde in dieses Zerwürfnis geraten war, gleichsam vernichtet (p.19).

'Gleichsam vernichtet', as if annihilated: these are strong words. They come like lightning from an almost cloudless sky to shatter the whole mood of peaceful, timeless beauty that Stifter has so carefully set up in the opening pages of the story. It is the first of many such inexplicable reversals of fortune we shall be meeting with in *Bunte Steine*. Even if we allow for the fact that the room had just been scrubbed clean, the mother's reaction was quite out of proportion to the actual part the boy played in the incident, in which he was the victim of a passing whim of mischievousness on the part of the normally kind pedlar of cart grease. The force of her phrase: 'You imp of the Devil!' ('Was hat denn dieser heillose, eingefleischte Sohn heute für Dinge an

[7] SW, XXV, p.179.

sich?' (p.18)) rings in the boy's ears like a religious commination, an excommunicating anathema. Equally elemental in its power is the following incident, where the comedy heightens the horror, when the mother in her fury covers everything with the pitch. We are made to feel as we see the black marks on the white floor that some hidden terror has been unleashed in the woman by which she is totally possessed.

We do not have to be soaked in the New Testament to think we are hearing the comforting words of Jesus when the grandfather says with a smile, 'So komme nur her zu mir, komme mit mir' (p.20). If we had any doubts, the following washing of the feet incident would tell us of the effect Stifter was here trying for. But the central point of the whole story is first indicated in another apparently trifling incident when the grandfather notices that the boy's shoes keep slipping on the short grass. It is only when we read the story for the second time that we realise how much Stifter has packed into every syllable of the old man's advice:

> Du mußt mit den Füßen nicht so schleifen; auf diesem Grase muß man den Tritt gleich hinstellen, daß er gilt, sonst bohnt man die Sohlen glatt und es ist kein sicherer Halt möglich. Siehst du, alles muß man lernen, selbst das Gehen. Aber komm, reiche mir die Hand, ich werde dich führen, daß du ohne Mühsal fortkömmst (p.30).

Given to a child, this advice is practical and pointed. But Stifter is concerned to lift our minds to the heights of such phrases as, 'Master, we know that thou art true, and teachest the way of God in truth'. We are not far distant from the use of religious parable.

The story is also a parable of education: how to teach and how to learn. And also of *what* has to be learnt. In this tale it is the history of the valley and the incidence of the plague. From the first steps of the walk the grandfather engages the boy's interest in his surroundings, lets him show off his knowledge of the locality, keeps his mind alert by pointing out many points of interest, big and small, important and unimportant, but all within the boy's powers of comprehension. He eventually comes to accept his grandfather's words as truth because he finds them confirmed by what he sees about him.

> Ich hatte Gelegenheit, als wir weiter gingen, die Wahrheit dessen zu beobachten, was der Großvater gesagt hatte. Ich sah eine Menge der weißgelben Blümlein auf dem Boden, ich sah den grauen Rasen, ich sah auf manchem Stamme das Pech wie goldene Tropfen stehen, ich sah die unzähligen Nadelbüschel auf den unzähligen Zweigen gleichsam aus winzigen dunklen Stiefelchen herausragen, und ich hörte, obgleich kaum ein Lüftchen zu verspüren war, das ruhige Sausen in den Nadeln (p.24).

The intervention of the plague story in this scene of beauty has something of the sudden onset of disaster about it akin to the unexpected punishment of the unsuspecting child.

> 'In allen diesen Wäldern und in allen diesen Ortschaften hat sich einst eine merkwürdige Tatsache ereignet, und es ist ein großes Ungemach über sie gekommen. Mein Großvater, dein Ururgroßvater, der zu damaliger Zeit gelebt hat, hat es uns oft erzählt. Es war einmal in einem Frühlinge, da die Bäume kaum ausgeschlagen hatten, da die Blütenblätter kaum abgefallen waren, daß eine schwere Krankheit über diese Gegend kam und in allen Ortschaften, die du gesehen hast, und auch in jenen, die du wegen vorstehender Berge nicht hast sehen können, ja sogar in den Wäldern, die du mir gezeigt hast, ausgebrochen ist. Sie ist lange vorher in entfernten Ländern gewesen und hat dort unglaublich viele Menschen dahingerafft. Plötzlich ist sie zu uns hereingekommen. Man weiß nicht, wie sie gekommen ist ...' (p.27).

It is especially in that last phrase that we come upon Stifter's belief that our lives, however well ordered, peaceful and regulated they may appear, are at any time prone to destruction, and that it is in those moments of catastrophe that man's real character, his real being, is exposed. Like a drum-beat under the account of the onset of the plague: 'Die Nachricht verbreitete sich in der Gegend, die Menschen erschraken und rannten gegen einander' (p.27), and when death began to take its toll: 'Die Kinder liebten ihre Eltern nicht mehr und die Eltern die Kinder nicht, man warf nur die Toten in die Grube und ging davon' (p.28), we may think we hear the muted message Stifter was getting from the disintegration of his beloved Austria.

On three separate occasions the grandfather talks of the plague, how it came, how people behaved, how they fled in panic, how they suffered and died. Each time the narration is interrupted by references to the present or by chance events such as the ringing of the bells or their visit and rest on the 'Machthof'. In this way an elaborate time sequence is suggested, as the grandfather tells of the times of *his* grandfather to give the boy something to remember and hand down to future generations. We thus get a folk memory spanning many generations. While this folk memory is a repository of the sterling qualities of a race, it is inevitably also a record of the race's capacity for evil. Stifter never blinked at this unwelcome truth. As he wrote in a tale entitled *Zuversicht*, first published in 1845, 'wir Alle haben eine tigerartige Anlage, so wie wir eine himmlische haben, und wenn die tigerartige nicht geweckt wird, so meinen wir, sie sei gar nicht da, und es herrsche blos die himmlische'.[8] The plague was for Stifter only one of the violent eruptions in society which released in man those darker passions which Stifter saw as wholly destructive, as we may see in the following extract from a newspaper article, which he wrote in April 1848: 'Die Leidenschaft strebt nach Thierischem, sei es die Erfüllung einer Körperempfindung (Wollust), sei es die Gewalt oder Alleingeltendmachung (Herrschsucht, Eifersucht, diese furchtbaren Geister der Menschheit, die sie leider mit dem Thiere, z.B. dem Hunde, gemein hat), und in diesem Streben aufgehalten, wird sie zum fanatischem Affecte, der blind gegen die Schranke stürmt.'[9] The grandfather, however, only hints at

[8] SW, XIII/2, p.492.

[9] SW, XVI, p.15.

these dark forces and emphasises the peace and contentment which returned to the region after the plague.

In the third, much more detailed and longer, account of the plague the boy is instructed how to bear himself when such calamities return. The grandfather, who had told the boy that on slippery grass he must put his feet down firmly and deliberately to show he meant it, now describes how a pitchburner's son 'vielleicht gerade so groß ... wie du' (p.38) both triumphed over his loneliness and desolation and earned himself the 'Waldmädchen mit den feinen Haaren'. When he comes to the painful parts of this narrative, Stifter changes his leisurely style to one more suited to the harsh facts. Such is the moment when the boy 'lief ... von der Hütte weg, weil er den toten Mann und das tote Weib entsetzlich fürchtete' (p.38). What a few hours before had been 'Vater und Mutter' are now horrifyingly changed, stripped of their identity, only distinguishable by their sex: 'der tote Mann, das tote Weib.'

Stifter took a great risk when he chose for the supreme test of the boy's qualities the most improbable coincidence of discovering a little girl lying unconscious in the undergrowth. But it was a conscious risk, and the author employs all his art to convert us to the view that it was not blind chance but a stroke of providential grace that brought about the meeting. We may speak of conscious art with some confidence because we have an earlier version of this story, which appeared in 1843 as *Die Pechbrenner*. In the final version we see that Stifter has shortened the detailed account of the girl and concentrated the horror of her fate in one phrase 'es hatte wirre Haare, und lag so ungefüg in dem Gestrüppe, als wäre es hineingeworfen worden' (p.39). And when his publisher showed him some sketches for the first edition of *Bunte Steine*, Stifter protested at the artist's attempt to disguise the horror of the bodily posture of the girl, thrown as it were on the dustheap like a discarded doll, and discarded before she had time to die.

The girl's plight arouses in the boy all those 'Kräfte' Stifter wrote about in his Preface, 'Kräfte, die nach dem Bestehen des Einzelnen zielen' (p.9). For through trying to save her and value her as the *Kleinod* of the *Vorrede* he manages to save himself.

For Stifter convinces us that the boy had given up all hope of
survival. 'Der Knabe war nun allein in dem fürchterlichen
großen Walde ... und da war jetzt überall niemand, niemand als
der Tod' (p.38). But roused by the even greater distress of the
little girl, he suddenly recalls that water and streams run down-
hill, that people live at the foot of the mountains, and that if he
follows the stream he must eventually get back to the survivors
of his village.

The reader who may have raised an eyebrow at the telling of
the boy's encounter in the primeval forest must steady himself
when he comes to the sequel which crowns the adventure. At a
first reading the introduction of such a fantastic ending seems an
alien intrusion on a narrative he had taken to be a disguised
sermon on practical morality. But when we go over the descent
from the desolate place, we may note at leisure that many difficulties and dangers that must be thought of as inevitable con-
comitants of such a feat are missing from the grandfather's tale.
We may then share something of Miranda's amazement when
she learns of the miraculous transportation to the magic isle and
her father's assurance that they were indeed 'blessedly holpe'
thither. But the return of the lost girl as a princess and the transformation of the poor pitch-burner's son into a 'Schloßherr'
suggests a more magical, fairy-tale power governing the young
people, something, if it may be so expressed, transcending
providence.

Stifter may have felt that such a sequel was in place since folk
memory does contain such pantomime-like transformation
scenes. This ending would lift the grandson's mind up to a world
of pure imagination, to a dream of golden gratification. But we
should not think of the boy's contentment as the sole purpose of
this astonishing sequel. For Stifter himself when a boy heard
many such *Märchen*, and as a grown man shared in the contemporary interest in folklore and the theories about it which set
the Grimm brothers off on their investigations. The use of the
magical to bring about a harmony in human affairs which the
ordinary working of a 'sanfte Gesetz' could never accomplish
was an extra weapon in his armoury Stifter could not resist.

A key to the symbolic import of Stifter's tale may be found in a feature of the style which often irritates the reader who is trying to follow the action. Surprising as it may sound, it is through the long, leisurely descriptions of landscapes, vegetation, and everyday objects that much of the symbolic meaning of his stories is revealed. An example will suggest how this key may be discovered and turned. The grandfather, who had been describing the measures taken by the pitch-burner to save himself and his family from the plague, interrupts his narrative to button his grandson's jacket as the evening has drawn in and become colder, before resuming with these words:

> 'Siehst du, mein liebes Kind,' fuhr er fort, 'es hat aber alles nichts geholfen, und es war nur eine Versuchung Gottes. Da die Büsche des Waldes ihre Blüten bekommen hatten, weiße und rote, wie die Natur will, da aus den Blüten Beeren geworden waren, da die Dinge, welche der Pechbrenner in die Walderde gebaut hatte, aufgegangen und gewachsen waren, da die Gerste die goldenen Barthaare bekommen hatte, da das Korn schon weißlich wurde, da die Haberflocken an den kleinen Fädlein hingen, und das Kartoffelkraut seine grünen Kugeln und blaulichen Blüten trug: waren alle Leute des Pechbrenners, er selber und seine Frau bis auf einen einzigen kleinen Knaben, den Sohn des Pechbrenners, gestorben' (pp.37f.).

The six occurrences of the word *da* fix the importance of the time relation in our minds. Each occurrence introduces a description of a small detail in the ripening process of nature. In this larger context there is careful gradation from the more general 'Büsche des Waldes, Blüten, Beeren', to the particular 'Gerste, Korn, Hafer, Kartoffeln', whose shapes and colours are conjured up with loving accuracy in minute detail, so that we seem to see them in front of us, or at least to be looking at a Dürer drawing of them, perfect in their rightness. 'Wie die Natur will', says Stifter, thus underlining the eternity of the process and contrasting it with the futility of the pitch-burner's efforts, setting the fullness and beauty of ripeness against the abrupt, aloof, undercutting of death.

When Stifter turns to the smaller details of everyday life, when, as in this example, he stoops over a sheaf of barley, he makes us believe that these small things are the things that matter; they represent a continuity, a duration that man with his inconstant nature can rarely achieve. When we have become absorbed in this characteristic feature of his style, we see that it is a direct expression of his views on man, nature, life and the universe. Every detail of his landscape descriptions is as laden with his philosophy as the minute detail in Bunyan's *Pilgrim's Progress*; that is to say the descriptions are not like botanic drawings, but are severely selective and subordinated to the artist's purpose. When you read his loving descriptions of the 'Kartoffelkraut', you think you can touch the plant, but when you compare it with the objective reality, you at once realise that important aspects are missing. Where are the insects which threaten the plants, where are the signs of wilting and fading, where is the smell of decay which is ever present where there has been flowering and thriving?

The same purposeful selectivity governs the accounts of the conditions of the two abandoned children in the primeval forest. Where were the wolves the grandfather still remembers from his own childhood? Where are the pangs of hunger the children must have felt on their frugal diet of berries, grains and potatoes? Did their clothes never tear, become smelly and rot? How was it that they met with no obstacles on their way down? Stifter makes it all sound so easy, almost a triumphal progress:

> Sie gingen an vielen Bäumen vorüber, an der Tanne mit dem herabhängenden Bartmoose, an der zerrissenen Fichte, an dem langarmigen Ahorne, an dem weißgefleckten Buchenstamme mit den lichtgrünen Blättern, sie gingen an Blumen, Gewächsen und Steinen vorüber, sie gingen unter dem Singen der Vögel dahin, sie gingen an hüpfenden Eichhörnchen vorüber oder an einem weidenden Reh (p.42).

The answer Stifter could make to all these questions might run like this: 'Your questions presuppose that my business was purely narrative, that my attitude towards the events was neutral and matter-of-fact. But who would have used six *da*'s to describe a cabbage patch? All my violent wrenches from the ordinary, flat methods of narration, such as those commonly favoured by writers of adventure stories, are not *fioriture*, they are not a plasterer's ornament intended to brighten up a dull exterior. It is in them that, if I may put it without blasphemy, I am about my Father's business. All these stylistic features of my prose are an integral part of my sacred mission. It is in them, it is by imposing them on the reader, by massaging his mind and subjecting it to my rhythms, that I ram home my moral: in *Granit*, such simple thoughts as 'weil das Gute größer ist als der Tod' (p.11); that the disinterested impulses of man will triumph over his innate egoism, that the stronger will help the weaker, that a stricken society can recover 'Maß' and a true balance of the claims of the individual and those of the community!'

Yet it is characteristic of all the tales in the *Bunte Steine* that, after we have taken in the author's last word on his moral purpose and have come to see his main aim to be to put before us a simple view of life and humanity, we are left with a wry aftertaste when we recall the numerous trailing loose ends or sombre undertones which tell us of a far less cheering side of life and of problems painful to contemplate which refuse to go away. If ever the dictum, 'never trust the artist, trust the tale' required exemplification, we could point to this collection. In *Granit*, for example, we may rightly feel that the incident with the mother is never resolved, for it is not enough to say, 'Aber lasse nur Zeit, sie wird schon zur Einsicht kommen, sie wird alles verstehen, und alles wird gut werden' (p.23). Her blessing at the end, we may feel, does not make up for her fury at the beginning.

The same may be true of the plague. Stifter's interpretation of its significance, both locally and universally, is not clear. In Christian times people were always sure that plagues were sent by God to punish mankind for palpable sins. They regularly returned to a verse in the Second Penitential Psalm: 'Day and night thy hand was heavy upon me.' And they also attributed to God the cessation of the punishment. The words 'Strafgericht' and 'Versuchung Gottes' were introduced by Stifter when he re-cast his story *Granit*, but he presents the arrival of the plague and its disappearance as inexplicable happenings. What could be more neutral as regards Christianity than this: 'aber es kamen wieder andere Tage, und die Gesundheit war wieder in unsern Gegenden' (p.43). It is a puzzling fact of Stifter's art that, although he goes out of his way to introduce powerful religious and biblical overtones, religion itself is kept strictly on the sidelines.

An even greater ambiguity rests like a cloud over Stifter's account of man's powers to learn from past mistakes. While on the one hand the grandfather confidently sets out to show the boy that he *can* fix items in his memory, he has also to tell him to what extent people in the past failed to learn by their past errors. 'Die Menschen vergessen gerne die alte Not und halten die Gesundheit für ein Gut, das ihnen Gott schuldig sei und das sie in blühenden Tagen verschleudern. Sie achten nicht der Plätze, wo die Toten ruhen, und sagen den Beinamen Pest mit leicht-fertiger Zunge, als ob sie einen anderen Namen sagten, wie etwa Hagedorn oder Eiben' (p.33). *Granit* is pervaded by the deeply pessimistic view that man does not change, cannot learn from history or his own past experience. Stifter cannot reconcile the two facts that, on the one hand man is capable of learning, and is therefore not a helpless victim to his lusts and passions so that 'er dem Thiere gegenüber nicht thierisch, sondern das schöne Bild eines Menschen sei',[10] yet keeps slipping back like the little boy on the slippery grass. The story, with its intricate time sequence, its strong emphasis on the experience of past generations, thus almost defeats its purpose.

In this context it is interesting to note that in the last para-graph of *Granit* Stifter presents us with a clear case of 'repression' as it is called in the works of Freud. The narrator remembers the grandfather's whole story including the fine hair of the girl, 'aber von den Pechspuren, die alles einleiteten, weiß ich nichts mehr, ob sie durch Waschen oder Abhobeln weg-gegangen sind, und oft, wenn ich eine Heimreise beabsichtigte, nahm ich mir vor, die Mutter zu fragen, aber auch das vergaß

[10] SW, XVI, p.161.

ich jedesmal wieder' (p.46). Is Stifter telling us here that man's memory must be selective and block the recurrence of those moments when the 'Entsetzliche, Zugrunderichtende' invades the personality? At the very least this last observation rekindles the reader's conviction that a final question hangs over this story and suggests that the idyllic harmony in which the story begins and with which it closes is at best precarious, at worst deceptive. Since despite all the grandfather's restorative efforts, the disruption of the family harmony has clearly left an indelible mark on the boy's sensitive soul, must we not conclude that for Stifter time is not a healer either for the individual or for the whole community?

If I have allowed the discussion of *Granit* an inordinate amount of space in such a short guide as this, it is not because I think that it deserves preferential treatment for its comparative artistic merit, but because I believe that Stifter gave it a special function as the opening tale of this collection of *Bunte Steine*. He clearly intended this narrative to be an important link with the *Vorrede* and to instruct the reader to discover how the rest of the stories are going to exemplify the leading ideas in the *Vorrede*. Stifter fulfils this function by the happy device of an old man instructing a young boy in the art of living and introducing him to the particular conditions that life imposes. This device allows Stifter a persuasive simplicity of thought and a natural naivety of tone, since everything the grandfather says is tailored to suit the psychological and intellectual needs and capacities of a child. Stifter avoids the pitfall of talking down to that level by making the old man such a respecter of the human dignity of the boy. We may feel at times that Stifter's urgent sense of a moral mission has got the bit within its teeth when the grandfather turns into too much of a Moses leading the chosen people out of the desert, but several features of his treatment of this narrator keep the missionary spirit within bounds and prevent the moral design from protruding in an unseemly fashion. The old man is given a solemn style and speaks in well shaped sentences. The boy's responses are almost ritual in their monotonous similarity. The relations between them are never stilted. The picture made by the two figures walking through the countryside with its changing light from the warm afternoon sun to the dusk of evening is kept alive throughout the whole story. They walk and talk, stop, look around and resume their walk till they come to rest on the large block of solid granite, smoothed and polished by generations of country people, from which the whole train of events began. Trees, houses, hills, forests and lakes are pointed out, and in the course of all this the reader's imagination is kindled until he becomes part of the proceedings without becoming aware of it. So, imperceptibly, he succumbs to Stifter's art and gives the grandfather some of the respect and awe he inspires in the boy.

This, I think, is what Stifter was working for in all these *Bunte Steine*. No doubt it gave him a freer hand to have so much of the message delivered to a young person. For he was able to show in an attractive way the truth of his cherished idea that, as in a chain of cause and effect, restorative moral forces are called forth in man when he is confronted with a suffering victim of another's unrestrained egoism. By choosing the miraculous turn he gives to the fate of the young plague victims, Stifter gratifies an inborn longing for harmony which ordinary events will never supply. Stifter was not alone in regarding such a use of the miraculous, provided it does not clash too violently with our sense of probability, as a legitimate weapon in a work of moral propaganda. The slight relaxation of our strictest demands for verisimilitude which he persuades us to accept introduces a blur in our thoughts: we cannot pronounce, as theologians, that we meet with God's law in such miracles, but we can dream that such events might be part of a 'sanftes Gesetz'.

3. 'Bergkristall'

Similar considerations may have accounted for Stifter's transfer of *Bergkristall* from its original position as the third story in his first volume to the place it now occupies as the opening tale of the second volume of the first edition of *Bunte Steine*. For *Bergkristall* differs from *Kalkstein*, *Turmalin*, and *Katzensilber* and resembles *Granit* in concluding on a note of apparent harmony. The two stories have further points of similarity. In both we are made to dwell on the apparently miraculous rescue of two children from certain death. In both the idyllic note is strengthened by the choice of small village communities and a single family as their focal points. But whereas in *Granit* the cruelty practised by people during the plague percolates to us through such a distance in time that we take it in as if part of some old local legend, the horrors that threaten the life of the two children in *Bergkristall* come over us with terrifying immediacy. There is also a difference in angle of perspective. In *Granit* man is shown to be the victim of the vicissitudes of fate, and his trials are sent to test him, whereas in *Bergkristall* Stifter is more concerned to make his moral points in terms of social criticism. He therefore lays bare the human failings which cause the disaster, faults of character whose origins lie as much in changes of social and economic position as in the inborn vices of all mankind. The reader is thereby forced to look both within to his own weaknesses and faults and to his own social and economic circumstances.

It is tempting to regard as an author's tip to the reader the opening reference to the celebration of Christ's nativity on Christmas Eve, the very day on which the children are lost on the mountain, telling us to see this as a clue to the interpretation of the whole story as essentially one of death and rebirth. Yet, once again, we find Stifter playing down the central mysteries of the faith which dominate the Christmas festival, and concentrating instead on the Yuletide aspects of conviviality and good cheer. One Christmas theme is immediately seen to be pointed: the willingness of the celebrants to come together at this time and forget their petty differences stands in marked contrast with the general picture Stifter paints of a narrow-minded, divided community.

Stifter's description is beautifully economic in its sarcasm: the villagers 'sind sehr stetig und es bleibt immer beim Alten. Wenn ein Stein aus einer Mauer fällt, wird derselbe wieder hinein-gesetzt, die neuen Häuser werden wie die alten gebaut, die schadhaften Dächer werden mit gleichen Schindeln aus-gebessert, und wenn in einem Hause scheckige Kühe sind, so werden immer solche Kälber aufgezogen, und die Farbe bleibt bei dem Hause' (p.142). Few visitors penetrate where there are only cart-tracks, the inhabitants therefore form a little world of their own, speak their own dialect, and are intimately aware of the smallest details of each other's doings in the present as well as the chronicle of past generations. As in many such claustro-phobic communities, a spirit of narrow clannishness develops. The cobbler's wife and her children are looked upon as foreigners. The intolerance of the villagers in Gschaid is matched by the arrogance of the Millsdorf master dyer on the other side of the pass.

Bergkristall too is a rewritten story. If we look back to the original version of 1845, entitled *Der heilige Abend*, the differences declare plainly Stifter's purpose in the revised version to contrast the stick-in-the-mud spirit of Gschaid with the desire to get on and 'better oneself' among the craftsmen who were trying by great personal exertions to develop their modest workshops into small factories. Stifter minutely examines the failings of both stagnation and progress as they are exhibited in the daily lives of these people and concentrates our attention on the unforeseen consequences of what may strike us at first as harmless misdemeanours; for example, a wrong weather forecast, a father's pride in exhibiting his children's strength and vigour, a wife's unquestioning dependence on her husband's authority, the neglect of a wooden pillar, etc.

Yet it is not from the subtlety and comprehensiveness of the social criticism that *Bergkristall* derives its power. It all comes from the mountain which towers above the village and makes the hamlet seem even smaller than it is. This power would have been lost if the mountain had been merely a symbol, for it is plainly because it is, by means of so many different treatments, made to seem what it *is* that the power grows as the story develops. Stifter describes this mountain six times in the course of the narrative. Its power lies in its inscrutable otherness, its immense remoteness from all the human activity which seeks, as it were, to humanise it and incorporate it into the villagers' way of life. The peasants may, as Stifter wrote, treat the mountain 'als hätten sie ihn selber gemacht' (p.142), but it remains ultimately separate and beyond their comprehension.

Nevertheless the mountain has this power because Stifter takes such trouble to make us see it in all its topographical and geological features, and in particular all the difficulties it presents to a would-be winter climber. The second of these descriptions is in some ways the most impressive (pp.143f.). For there Stifter describes the mountain as it presents itself in the changes of the seasons. He introduces us at once to all the wilder aspects, its 'Zacken, Gipfel, Hörner', each carefully differentiated to warn the mountain dwellers of a special danger. We hear of 'Abhänge, steilrechte Wände, Steilseiten, Bergfelder, Felsen, Kuppeln, Blöcke, Platten, Trümmer'. The repeated mention of 'Schnee, Winterschnee, Firm, Eis, Geschiebe von Eis, Eisfelder' and the dirty edge of the glacier with its boulders, rocks, bare earth and mud conjure up a vision of remote, desolate beauty. The mountain peaks 'stehen, wenn sie an hellen Tagen sichtbar sind, blendend in der finstern Bläue der Luft' (p.143) or 'ragen schwarz in den Himmel' (p.143). There is a strange, oscillating light playing over the ice and rocks which adds to the ominous fascination, the spell, of this great mass of a mountain which in winter 'wie ein Zauberpalast aus dem bereiften Grau der Wälderlast emporragt' (p.143).

But the awesome power of these descriptions would not work so well, of course, if there were no children to be exposed to death on the slopes. Stifter can match all these details with the confrontation between their puny strength and this immense wilderness of ice and snow. Stifter makes us feel the horror of their hopeless situation: 'Es waren riesenhaft große, sehr durcheinander liegende Trümmer, die mit Schnee bedeckt waren, der überall in die Klüfte hineinrieselte, und an die sie sich ebenfalls fast anstießen, ehe sie sie sahen. Sie gingen ganz hinzu, die Dinge anzublicken. Es war Eis — lauter Eis' (p.166). As the tension grows to unbearable anxiety, we are reminded of the horror confronting the Ancient Mariner:

> The ice was all between.
> The ice was here, the ice was there
> The ice was all around.

Page after page we watch the children climb, slide, fall, frustrated in every attempt to find a way out. The snow and ice are alive with colours; hidden horrors glint in the pale half-light. The children try to peer around them, 'aber es war rings um sie nichts als das blendende Weiß, überall das Weiß' (p.164). They try to catch a sound, 'aber sie hörten nichts' (p.164). In a highly suggestive, dramatic style, by means of repetition, variation, accumulation, and by stressing the various hues of white, grey, blue and black, the rugged contours, the strange shapes of the rocks, Stifter forces us to acknowledge the powerful, awe-inspiring, uncaring majesty of the mountain.

How then are the children saved?

Stifter refuses to treat the subject as a religious legend such as were so common in mountain regions where to this day many a roadside chapel, or a wooden pillar with a crudely painted picture like that of Stifter's 'Unglücksäule', or a clumsy carving on a rock face tell us how 'Maria half' by a miraculous escape from certain death by an avalanche or a fall of rocks. It is true that after her rescue Sanna says, 'Mutter, ich habe heute nachts, als wir auf dem Berge saßen, den heiligen Christ gesehen' (p.183), but Stifter is careful to counteract our natural assumption that he subscribed to the child's vision by his emphasis on the part played in the rescue by such natural phenomena as the cracking of the ice and the grandiose spectacle of the illuminated sky, which prevented the children from falling into a sleep from which they would never have awoken.

Ultimately Stifter leaves the question open and does not instruct us in how to interpret or relate the parts played by nature and what seems to us to amount to divine intervention. He seems to resort to a sort of pantheistic unity of both. Here are the two key sentences.

> In den fernen Ländern draußen waren unzählige Kirchen und Glocken, und mit allen wurde zu dieser Zeit geläutet, von Dorf zu Dorf ging die Tonwelle, ja man konnte wohl zuweilen von einem Dorfe zum andern durch die blätter-losen Zweige das Läuten hören: nur zu den Kindern herauf kam kein Laut, hier wurde nichts vernommen; denn hier war nichts zu verkündigen (p.174).

And the children would have fallen asleep, and so died 'wenn nicht die Natur in ihrer Größe ihnen beigestanden wäre und in ihrem Innern eine Kraft aufgerufen hätte, welche imstande war, dem Schlafe zu widerstehen' (p.174). On the surface these two sentences seem to contradict each other, yet, at the same time, they suggest a powerful link, the interpretation of which Stifter leaves as a challenge to his readers to reconcile by their own efforts if they can.

What would not have been an insurmountable difficulty for any cultivated Austrian in 1853 will be a stumbling block for many of his modern European readers. It is that in the world of his art Stifter entertained, and expected his readers to entertain, a number of quite different and ultimately incompatible views on all those large matters of which man can have no knowledge but which are of supreme concern to all men in their conduct of life and above all in the contemplation of death and a possible afterlife. Stifter expected his readers to suspend their allegiance to any *one* explanation of these ultimate problems and to give an almost impartial credence to rival beliefs. He wanted his readers to range from a vague pantheism, in which the Creator and the created are one, to the thought that nature does not need to be redeemed but only sinful man, or the view that Nature is a law unto herself, and quite separate from man's affairs.

The same ambiguity and complexity apply to the second sentence, which seems to suggest that Nature as a personified agent, almost as in a fairy-tale, helps the children to survive. Here it is essential to give the word 'beistehen' its full meaning. 'Jemandem beistehen' means 'jemandem, der in einer bestimmten Situation Hilfe braucht, stärken, aufrichten, stützen, durch sein Verhalten, mit Worten oder Taten, ihm die Möglichkeit geben, eine Krise zu überwinden; betont die Verbundenheit des Handelnden mit der in Not geratenen Person'. Nature, of course cannot break her own laws. The rescue is no miracle. The events which follow all occur in a perfectly natural way. But Nature is mysterious, and Stifter explicitly allows us to entertain a different interpretation which goes beyond the purely natural when he puts the question, was there another cause at work illuminating the heavens: '... oder war es eine andere Ursache der unergründlichen Natur' (p.175).

Stifter, it seems to me, is plainly suggesting that the children somehow deserved to be saved because instead of panicking they stuck together in their struggle for survival. Konrad, in particular, like the pitch-burner's son in *Granit*, displays resources of inner strength which allow him to care for his little sister, even though he can do so little. He is calm and sensible: he remembers that you must keep moving, and must not fall asleep. He makes good use of the grandmother's coffee extract and the other victuals she had packed in his bag. Nevertheless when we tot up all his efforts, which undoubtedly succeeded in prolonging their lives, we have to admit that by their own efforts they would never have found a way down. The meeting with the rescue party remains one of those miraculous coincidences that even in our day with our mountain-rescue planes and full-scale paramilitary operations we acknowledge as the one decisive factor whenever such a rescue succeeds. The normal thing, then as now, is for the rescuers to come upon dead bodies frozen stiff.

It is interesting to note that Stifter has taken pains to make this miraculous coincidence as plausible as possible. He has various speakers comment on the extraordinary absence of wind, which in the snowfall would have chilled the children to the marrow, buried them in snowdrifts, or blown them into a crevasse or off the mountain face. A sign of this care is a little change Stifter made in his revised version. In *Der heilige Abend* the children get down from the rock as soon as they catch sight of the rescuers and walk towards them (Jf. p.171). This would almost certainly have meant that they would have been lost from sight again. In the revised version Stifter has them standing still on the rock and thus maintaining visual contact until the rescuers could come up to them.

As in *Granit*, the children's descent down the mountain is almost triumphal. But this time Stifter introduces a realistic note by drawing on the Christian connotations of the holy time. When the rescue party who are bringing the children down hear the sacring bell announcing the elevation of the Host, they fall to their knees and give thanks to God. Stifter's word for the bell, 'Wandlungsglöcklein', seems to be full of promise, not only of the religious transubstantiation but also of the moral transformation of the villagers. Yet once again Stifter strangely qualifies the positive impact of the miraculous rescue by suggesting at the end that although the people of Gschaid now accept mother and children into their fold, there is no guarantee that they have fundamentally altered their attitude to the stranger in their midst. For these villagers the incident is soon reduced to the level of one of those tall stories about the mountain that they like to tell each other or to strangers, and even then, Stifter hints, it will only be a matter of time before they forget it completely. Only Konrad and Sanna will not forget the mountain and their experience on it when they look at the mountain from a safe distance 'und er so schön und so blau wie das sanfte Firmament auf sie herniederschaut' (p.184).

They are the only ones who have understood at least something of the mysterious otherness of nature. But as the lovely peaceful Sunday morning in *Granit* only covers up the lurking threat of perpetual conflict from within and without, so in *Bergkristall* the beautiful sunshine, the scent of flowering linden-trees and the humming of bees are ultimately deceptive. The fact that Stifter makes no mention again of the human failings and the social evils that led to the children facing death on the icy slopes of the mountain does not mean that these problems have gone away by themselves or have been even tentatively solved. As in *Granit* the promise of hope is restricted to the limited sphere of the particular case and its scope severely curtailed by the passing of time and man's imperfect memory. Stifter is much too much of a realist and fine observer of life to pretend that he has a panacea in his art for the ills of the world. Yet in these two stories — at least for a short time and within the narrow confines of their setting — he allows the good to prevail over the bad as a sign that there is some hope as long as man does not close his mind completely to the need for constant vigilance. This is the reason, I would like to suggest, that he gave these two stories the important function of opening the first and second volumes of this collection. They engender in the reader the feeling that perhaps there is a point in trying to keep alert and become aware of the dangers that imperceptibly but surely bedevil the life of the individual and of society as a whole.

4. 'Kalkstein'

No tale in *Bunte Steine* asks so much from the reader as *Kalkstein*. No other invites him, and indeed forces him, to travel further into unfamiliar regions of the spirit than this. While it might be too bold to say that if ever a story by Stifter 'sorts the men from the boys' it is this, or that the history of criticism of this tale is strewn with the corpses of those who have taken a part for the whole, it cannot be denied that many previous commentators have failed to resist the temptation of a facile solution or to discover in what respects this is the finest story in the collection. This being so, it will be as well to begin with a general appraisal before setting out the detailed steps by which Stifter leads us into the heart of his mystery.

In *Kalkstein* Stifter is celebrating man in as paradoxical a way as Shakespeare did when he made Hamlet say:

> What a piece of work is a man, how noble in reason, how infinite in faculties, in form and moving how express and admirable, in action how like an angel, in apprehension how like a god: the beauty of the world, the paragon of animals,

in the very breath with which he continues:

> and yet to me, what is this quintessence of dust?

For, if I am not mistaken, Stifter never came nearer to exhibiting the real mystery of human nature and what constitutes its grandeur than when he chose to celebrate man in a person who in most people's eyes would be branded a failure or a neurotic or even a damned soul. The story is thus the most daring vindication of the claim Stifter was making in his *Vorrede* that the most important matters of life are to be found in the apparently simplest and unimportant events of obscure lives, 'in Unzahl wiederkehrenden Handlungen der Menschen' (p.11). For at the death of an insignificant priest there emerges for the reader a thought which also occurs at the end of many tragedies, that what has just happened had to happen so, and has happened as a direct consequence of the working out of the laws of the universe which determine man's scope and his lot. So Stifter at the end brings us round with full comprehension to his opening remarks:

> Gott habe die Menschen erschaffen, wie er sie erschaffen habe, man könne nicht wissen, wie er die Gaben verteilt habe, und könne darüber nicht hadern, weil es ungewiß sei, was in der Zukunft in dieser Beziehung noch zum Vorschein kommen könne (p.47).

By the end, these prophetic phrases have acquired their maximum weight. When we understand the futility of searching for a cheerful moral in this tale, all thoughts of the 'sanfte Gesetz' drop away as finally irrelevant.

The first step towards an understanding of *Kalkstein* is made when we eventually come to see that our principal witness and informant is the first to take the tale for an album piece of sweet consolation. With all the finesse of a skilled detective-story writer Stifter leads us first into the error of thinking the surveyor a man of sense and of judgement far surpassing that of the poor Catholic priest. This surveyor has all the detective hero's acumen in pouncing on the incongruous feature of the priest's dress and in following up the clues which reveal the strange obsession with fine linen which he tries to hide from the world. It is only gradually, as we learn more of the priest's life, that it dawns on us that the surveyor is a coarse fellow by comparison and quite incapable of appreciating the finer mould and more exquisite apprehensions of the suffering priest. Indeed, he crassly supposes that he understands why the priest was ashamed of keeping this linen, and after his death he purchases the best bits:

Auch ich erwarb etwas in der Versteigerung ... sämtliche

noch übrigen so schönen und feinen Leinentücher und
Tischtücher. Ich und meine Gattin besitzen die Sachen
noch bis auf den heutigen Tag ... Wir bewahren sie als ein
Denkmal auf, daß der arme Pfarrer diese Dinge aus einem
tiefen dauernden und zarten Gefühle behalten und nie
benutzt hat (p.101).

Stifter scrupulously leaves the interpretation to the reader. It will
be the critic's task by careful analysis to demonstrate that what
places this story above such an excellent tale as Melville's
Bartleby the Scrivener is that the true reasons for the priest's
secrecy are far more complicated and far less blameless than the
coarse-grained surveyor supposed. 'There are more things in
heaven and earth', we must say to the surveyor and to all those
who think he is here the author's mouthpiece, 'than are dreamt
of in your philosophy'.

Yet it is precisely this idea — a stroke of genius I am tempted
to call it — to present the priest through the eyes of the surveyor,
that gives Stifter all the freedom he wishes to manipulate the
reader's reactions to the story. It allows him to offer or withhold
at will insights into the priest's nature, thus all the time forcing
the reader to compare his own responses with the surveyor's. By
making his narrator a surveyor, used to observing closely and in
detail the lie of the land, and with a factual, scientific approach
to all that meets his eyes, Stifter has expertly chosen a convincing and realistically acceptable contrast to the figure of the
gentle priest, imperfectly at home with the practical sides of life.
Yet to think of the surveyor as an objective and reliable guide,
registering everything with true scientific detachment, would be
to disregard Stifter's deliberate characterisation of the narrator.

The surveyor, immediately on taking up the narration, introduces himself as a man of standing, a trained surveyor, a civil
servant, who is proud of his profession and motivated by
ambition to work hard and efficiently. 'Gewöhnlich', in the
sense of 'traditional, customary, conventional, usual, normal',
is one of his favourite epithets, denoting the stance of an
individual who is well integrated into a society that expects from
a man of his education and position a definite, clear-cut outlook

on life, firm reactions and settled points of view. Nevertheless he is occasionally allowed to deviate a little but never to depart from them completely. Stifter portrays him as a kindly man, not insensitive to the changing hues of the skies and the beauty of the landscape, although he admits to being attracted more by a grandiose romantic wilderness than by the gentler aspects of nature. He also has an eye for the idiosyncracies of human nature and a heart large enough to be moved by them, even to the extent of disrupting the daily routine of his work when the priest falls ill. Stifter not only gives him a pair of sharply observant eyes and an excellent memory but also the gift of turning his observations into precise, vivid, highly visual and evocative descriptions.

Yet for all this, his limitations are clearly delineated. At the beginning of the narrative, in describing the dinner party and the various people sitting round the table, he uses the phrase, 'Nur ein einziger Gast war nicht zu erkennen' (p.48). 'Erkennen' here has more the sense of 'allocating to a definite social context, to a known sphere of experience' than the usual meaning of 'recognising'. Although not immune to the gentle appeal of the humble priest's peculiarities and the striking clarity of his blue eyes, what excites the surveyor's curiosity more than anything else is the priest's threadbare clothes, the dull, faded colours. They do not fit into his comfortable views of what a priest should look like, as he reflects again later when he comes across the priest in the Kar Valley:

> Die ungemeine Armut, wie ich sie noch niemals bei einem Menschen oberhalb des Bettlerstandes angetroffen habe, namentlich nicht bei solchen, die andern als Muster der Reinlichkeit und Ordnung vorzuleuchten haben, schwebte mir beständig vor. Zwar war der Pfarrer beinahe ängstlich reinlich, aber gerade diese Reinlichkeit hob die Armut noch peinlicher hervor und zeigte die Lockerheit der Fäden, das Unhaltbare und Wesenlose dieser Kleidung (pp.52f.).

This sentence is an example of the masterly way Stifter uses the

surveyor not only to convey certain observations and
impressions to the reader but also to implant thoughts in his
mind which the surveyor himself fleetingly entertains but never
pursues. In the example at hand, this is the short phrase 'beinahe
ängstlich reinlich', which hints at the possibility of some psychological obsession, and is aimed at raising a question in the
reader's mind while the surveyor, not much given to musings,
and who never probes beyond the surface even of his own
observations, never refers to it again. The surveyor's comment
on the priest's frilly cuffs and the furtive movements with which
he tries to push them back betrays a similarly restricted
approach, dictated by his own outlook: 'Vielleicht waren sie in
einem Zustande, daß er sich ihrer hätte ein wenig schämen
müssen' (p.49), a thought that obviously bothered him a great
deal, for he takes it up again much later in the story, when he
visits the priest in his house, and sees the fine linen, 'Ich machte
daher genauere Beobachtungen und kam darauf, daß er sich
seiner Handkrausen keineswegs zu schämen habe' (p.54).
Although the surveyor never radically changes his first
impression of the priest, Stifter adds to the interest of the
characterisation by showing that up to a point the surveyor is
capable of modifying his initial judgements.

One of Stifter's means of bringing this out is the surveyor's
changing attitude to the landscape. Initially, all his sympathies
are with the gardens and orchards surrounding Schauenberg.
The craggy limestone area of the Kar Valley is for him 'eine
abscheuliche' (p.52), 'eine fürchterliche Gegend' (p.50), dull,
unattractive, without any dramatic scenery. Although he prides
himself on his power of observation, it is only under the priest's
gentle guidance that he learns to appreciate the hidden beauty of
the bleak surroundings. At the end, when he leaves the valley,
having successfully completed his surveying, he is surprised at
his own reactions. 'Eines sehr seltsamen Gefühles muß ich
Erwähnung tun, das ich damals hatte. Es ergriff mich nämlich
beinahe eine tiefe Wehmut, als ich von der Gegend schied,
welche mir, da ich sie zum ersten Male betreten hatte, abscheu-
lich erschienen war' (pp.94f.). The conversion, however, is not
total, as his formulation, the grudging 'nämlich beinahe' makes

clear. His scientific frame of mind and complacent bourgeois outlook are at odds with his inner awakening.

Stifter suggests by various means, which emphasise the similarity of the priest and his environment, that we must take the surveyor's attitude to the Kar as symbolically representative of his relation to the priest. We are made to feel that an affinity exists between the unique features of the priest and the special character of the stone valley. Stifter underlines this by colour symbols relating to both. The muted hues of the priest's shabby clothes, that caught the surveyor's eye in the first instance, reappear in the stones and the colouring of the valley, and it hardly needs the striking picture of the priest sitting on a heap of sand, 'Er hatte seine großen Schuhe fast in den Sand vergraben, und auf den Schößen seines Rockes lag Sand' (p.51), to bring out his oneness with the landscape he has come to love and understand. Although it is through him that we acquire visual knowledge, the surveyor is no more than dimly aware of the significance and interrelation of what he reports.

Stifter has thus created for himself in the figure of the narrator a wonderful way of impressing on the reader's mind in the most vivid and realistic detail all he wants him to know about the kind of environment the clergyman moves in without ever having to change the narrative viewpoint or to interrupt its flow by stepping forward himself in giving the necessary objective detail. In fact the reader never receives objective direction. He comes to look at everything through the eyes of the surveyor, to experience and even to think the way he does. We have, without our being aware of it, been made to erect two orders of being. One may be called the common-sense and merely commonplace view of what is right and proper, aptly summed up in the word 'gewöhnlich'. The other, by contrast, stands condemned because it is seen only as a failure to match the 'gewöhnlich'. It will be Stifter's task in the rest of the story to upset this scale of judgement, to shift the fundamental values of the whole tale.

Stifter thus manipulates the reader's susceptibilities without him — at least at first — realising this. It is only when we discover with what slight touches of irony the surveyor is presented by Stifter that we cease to regard his value judgements as necessarily final. Critical awakening, I should imagine, will occur at different places for different readers. The whole story is shot through with subtle observations of the surveyor's deep-rooted obtuseness, his easy satisfaction with his powers of instant recognition and, last but not least, of his love of food and his pride in the skill with which he manages to provide himself with creature comforts even in the remote Kar region.

It is with the dramatic impact of the thunderstorm that all readers must pass an instant review of all the favourable impressions they had formed of this astute surveyor. It is with something of a shock that we discover that in the surveyor's own field of scientific observation of atmospheric conditions, he is no match for the priest's intuitive knowledge of the imperceptible signs of the imminent change of weather. (This clearly is one of Stifter's constants in judging characters in many *Bunte Steine* stories.) The scene during the thunderstorm is a sustained exercise by Stifter in contrasting the two so essentially different men. A great part of what may appear merely as a display of Stifter's outstanding powers of description, is in fact an invitation to the reader to make damning discriminations between the finest and coarsest traits in human nature.

Stifter puts the whole description of the storm in the mouth of the surveyor whose love for the grandiose in nature finds fulfilment in the slashing rain, reverberating thunderclaps and strange light-effects of the lightning flashes. When rewriting the original version of the story *Der arme Wohltäter* Stifter much enlarged the description of the storm and emphasised the attitude of concentrated listening in the two men, who in *Der arme Wohltäter* are actually eating their frugal meal while thunder, lightning and rain surround the house. By this shift in emphasis Stifter makes us aware that the storm has a different meaning for the two men. While the surveyor listens with awe-inspired admiration, the priest shows the attitude of someone who accepts the violent forces, calmly submitting to them, but relieved when they pass, as his simple words 'Es ist vorüber', echoing the 'missa est' of the mass, indicate (p.59).

The storm brings the two men closer, as any shared experience of that magnitude would, but it also accentuates their differences. Stifter ironically explores these differences further by showing how deeply, even in recalling the events, the surveyor is discomforted by the frugal meal that follows, the almost ritualistic manner with which it is served, and the priest's preparations for the night. Although the surveyor keeps protesting out of politeness and a genuine concern for the priest's poverty that he is used to putting up with simple provisions and spartan sleeping quarters, all the details he notices and recalls point to his great amazement at what he witnesses. And it is the amazement of a well-fed, pampered person, who, even in rough surroundings, expects a certain level of material comfort. Stifter brings out the surveyor's impercipience about the priest's unique personality and lifestyle by the devastating description of the way he displays his packed lunch and eating utensils. The episode unrolls in front of our eyes as if in slow motion. We are appalled at the surveyor's hearty, unthinking and crude behaviour. As soon as he begins to lay them out, we see how inappropriate it was to display the 'Scheibchen von feinem weißen Weizenbrote ... Scheibchen von Schinken, von kaltem Braten und Käse ...', not to mention good wine and the elaborate wine-cooler (p.60). We form our verdict on his crass behaviour long before this dawns on him. We realise the limitations of his understanding and come to see what he calls in retrospect euphemistically 'Übereilung', impolite rashness (p.61), as something much more serious, a fundamental insensitivity. Stifter enlarges on the theme of insensitivity when the surveyor recalls how his indiscreetly questioning glances made the priest blush about his fine linen sheets. All the religious implications of the priest's ritual acts which are duly reported by the surveyor and therefore are noted by the reader, completely escape his comprehension.

Further examples begin to accumulate rapidly to show that Stifter is deliberately forcing the reader to perceive the essential difference of the two spiritual orders of being which we are now beginning to glimpse. One such example, that surely dispels the presumption that the same common love of children unites the two men, is the surveyor's horrified reaction at the priest's assumption that he had come to render active help in guiding the children through the murky flood water. 'Ich erschrak über diese Zumutung, sagte aber gleich, ich sei eben nicht zur Hilfe herbeigeeilt, da ich nicht gewußt hätte, daß Kinder über den Steg kommen würden, aber wenn Hilfe nötig geworden wäre, so würde ich sie gewiß auch geleistet haben' (p.69). This is an excellent illustration of Stifter's artistic skill. The surveyor's words characterise him as deeply conventional. The thought of having to step into the water appals him, yet he does not want to be outshone by the priest. His whole behaviour reflects the normal; we would not have reacted very differently ourselves. This forces the reader to reflect not only on the surveyor's behaviour but also on the whole scene of the priest standing hip-deep in the shining watery expanse with the children wading up to him, which Stifter has built up with such heavy symbolic overtones of baptism or of the biblical 'Suffer the little children to come unto me, and forbid them not, for of such is the kingdom of God'. The surveyor's remarks reveal both his own failure to rise to the occasion but also the essentially extraordinary, even eccentric aspects of the priest's undertaking. We now begin to sense that the heavens are opening, and that, however many causes are going to be given as having governed the priest's life, the answers to the questions raised are never going to be adequate to our growing conviction that we are touching upon an inexhaustible mystery, but a mystery not of the queer sides, but of the essentially human sides of life. We now begin to reinterpret the word 'unusual' in a positive sense. But at these moments, when we seem to be seeing things more clearly, we find ourselves wrestling with a deep ambiguity; for while there is more than a hint of mystery, there is a strong suggestion of radical ambiguity which no amount of re-reading could ever uproot. Could we, for instance, give the priest a clean bill of spiritual health covering all his concern for and interest in the welfare of the children?

The challenge to go beyond the easily discernible applies also to the priest's account of his early life, the one long passage in the story where the intermediary role of the narrator is reduced to that of a passive listener, and Stifter enables us to gauge our own responses to the priest's story without first having to take the surveyor's reactions into account. It is, however, quite wrong to assume that the narrator totally disappears from the scene. He figures prominently as the recipient of the priest's account. Twice, at the beginning and at the end of his account, the priest stresses that he is telling the surveyor his life's story to put him into a position to understand 'Wie alles so gekommen ist, was jetzt ist' (p.75) and to make him more inclined to act as the executor of his will. His formulations reveal that he sees some pattern of cause and effect in his life which he hopes will sound convincing to the surveyor and explain 'wie es noch ... ist' (p.92). Yet the reader who expects at this point to be given an answer to his many questions is sorely disappointed. The priest's words are so muted, his narration so disjointed that one wonders whether he found it too painful or was himself quite unable to be more explicit. Yet the surveyor's satisfied 'Ich wußte nun, weshalb er sich seiner herrlichen Wäsche schämte' (p.92) is only adequate within the narrow circle of his enquiry, which to a large extent was still dictated by his strong impressions on first meeting the priest. The priest's story at least enabled the surveyor to place him in a certain social context, to explain his poverty and the existence of the fine linen. 'Es wäre gar zu traurig, wenn ich die Wäsche weggeben müßte' (p.92) says the priest. The surveyor takes these elusive words at their face value, and interprets the priest's reluctance to part with his linen as the sentiments of a man who could never quite forget his first and only love affair, a notion which by its very sentimentality fits into his conventional expectations. What he totally ignores is that by answering simple questions the priest's story raises a multitude of others in the reader's mind as he seems to discern a pattern of cause and effect only to see it disappear into nothingness.

The areas of problems and questions to which we get no clear answer are exclusively concerned with the inner life of a member of a hard-working and practical family who virtually opts out of this activity and progressively isolates himself. The priest's account of his own personal fate within this family is a disturbing exercise in self-restraint and understatement. So much is merely hinted at, has to be read between the lines and elaborated from a telling phrase or terse sentence, that one feels Stifter is using this method deliberately to force us to entertain many different ideas, and finally to realise that there is no one single but many complex reasons explaining 'wie alles so gekommen ist' (p.75), as he puts it.

Although the priest makes light of it, the appalling fact which emerges is the lovelessness of his upbringing. He not only lost his mother at birth but none of the other members of the family ever really cared for him. It seems to me that this is one of the cardinal points in the whole story of *Kalkstein*. There are no recollections of family intimacies. What looms large in the priest's memory are his learning difficulties and the figure of the tutor from whom there was no escape. 'Wir fuhren oft mit unsern Schimmeln durch die Stadt, wir fuhren auch auf das Land oder sonst irgendwo herum, und der Lehrer saß immer bei uns in dem Wagen' (p.79). The boy's education fails lamentably. He is not steered towards self-reliance and self-respect, which Stifter sees as the true goal of education. From Stifter's wording it is evident that the boy's difficulties are emotional rather than academic. Stifter is not specific about the reasons. There is the obvious one: the able brother who knows how to please. But the trouble seems more deep-seated — a sense of guilt, perhaps, that he caused the mother's death, the father's loneliness? He seems to accept it as somehow 'just' and 'deserved' that the brother is given more authority. Again, one is left in doubt about his real feelings on the matter. Is he glad to be cast aside, thus avoiding a heavy load of responsibilities, or is he only meek and gentle because he feels this is expected of him? He seems unable to make the step from childhood to manhood. Although when left untrammelled by direct competition, he is able to succeed in his studies, yet the idea of proving himself by going over missed ground, aimlessly at first till the brother suggests a goal, is backward-looking and puerile.

It is against this background of inadequacy that we must see the love affair — if one can call it that — with the young girl from next door. Of all the episodes in the story this is by far the most ambiguous. It has been seen on the one hand as an example of purest love (*20*, p.20 and *23*, p.77), and on the other, as an illustration of the tiger-like nature of man (*22*, p.250; p.245), and although both accounts are one-sided, Stifter might be held responsible for both, the reason being the total indetermination of the whole narrative, that is to say, there is no single detail which gives us an unequivocal clue as to what is really happening.

For example: 'Ich sah es gar so gerne an' (p.87) — says the priest. 'Es' refers to 'ein Töchterlein, ein Kind, nein, es war doch kein Kind mehr — ich wußte eigentlich damals nicht, ob es noch ein Kind sei oder nicht' (p.86). Much has been made of this uncertainty, as if the young man was trying to seduce a child under the age of consent. But if we read the sentence carefully, we see that the priest says 'damals'. Should we believe him? Was he really too inexperienced at the time to define her age? Much speaks for this interpretation: his solitary life, his upbringing, his general ill-adjustment to the practicalities of life. But we cannot be sure. The subtlety of the situation and formulation forbids any simple conclusion. There is, however, the fact that the girl very soon afterwards gets married, and must therefore have reached nubile age, which in those days could have been as early as sixteen.

But ambiguities remain. This is also true of the strange gift of the peach. On the one hand, it can be seen as nothing more sinister than the clumsy first attempt of a little boy of five or six to win the favours of the little girl in a white pinafore whom he meets in the playground and whose golden curls excite a strange longing in him. On the other hand, the beautifully rounded peach brings Eve's apple to mind. Three times the young man stretches his hand through the garden railings to place the peach carefully in the girl's path. 'Beim dritten Male blieb ich stehen, als der Pfirsich mit seiner sanften roten Wange auf dem Sande lag, und sagte, da sie in die Nähe kam: "Nimm ihn"' (p.87). Stifter's scene-setting, the use of traditional symbols, familiar to us all, like the apple or the garden of Eden, gives food for thought, yet again could mean no more than that, rather belatedly, the young man is overcome by the kind of uncontrollable feelings which rightly belong to the age of puberty, feelings which he does not fully understand and does not know how to channel in a more realistic direction. His hovering in the bushes might be taken to be akin to the lewdness of the Susanna story in the Bible, yet could be just as well the action of a young boy unsure of himself. Stifter must want us to think of all these possibilities. They are all present, different shades of the same spectrum. To single one out as a secure basis for interpretation would, I think, detract from Stifter's intentions to make us feel acutely the very complex and intricate nature of his subject.

We meet the same subdued hues of many possible meanings in the young man's strange interest in the beautiful 'weiße Tücher and andere Wäsche' (p.85) which he sees hanging in the neighbour's garden and of which he says, 'ich hatte die weißen Dinge sehr lieb' (p.87). The whole emphasis on cleaning and cleansing, on the girl's part, too, opens all sorts of speculations which are never going to be focused or fulfilled. What Stifter wants us to take in and ponder are not the realistic details but the emotional stresses and strains in a sensitive human being: the existence side by side, perhaps, of a longing for purity, and pure love, and the sexual desires that threaten this longing from within. Any normal young man, normal by the generally laid down standards of our society, would have cut through the Gordian knot, found his way round the garden railings and asked for the girl's hand in marriage, thus putting the seal of respectability on his conflicting desires. The tanner's son is incapable of such rationalisation — perhaps his general sense of failure prevents it, perhaps his inner need for purity, or on the contrary, the welling-up of an overwhelming desire which he is unable to contend with. The effect of the mother's 'Johanna, schäme dich' (p.88), seems to point to the latter reason, especially the formulation which the priest uses to describe his emotions and which is strikingly close to Genesis, chapter 3: 'Wir schämten uns wirklich und liefen auseinander. Mir brannten die Wangen vor Scham, und ich wäre erschrocken, wenn mir jemand im Garten begegnet wäre' (p.88). The young man never again emerges from the bushes where he is hiding. For the thoroughly involved reader his buying and hoarding of silver and linen makes extremely painful reading, for we are finally persuaded that he will never become a man.

As in *Granit* and *Bergkristall*, we come across one of those terse formulations with which Stifter indicates an almost traumatic experience like the one he remembers from his own childhood. 'Ich meinte damals, daß ich mir die Seele aus dem Körper weinen müsse' (p.89), says the priest, but it still needs the collapse of the family firm, the death of the brother and utter loneliness before he decides to 'have a go', to find a purpose and a meaning in life.

But here we feel that there is no symbolic rightness about this sudden turn to disaster. It is an arbitrary twist which allows Stifter to isolate his main figure. Although he becomes a servant of God, we ought not to put his entry into the priesthood down to a deep religious awakening. It is in keeping with the impression we have that the tanner's son all along evades responsibilities. There is no suggestion that he embraces the celibate life of a priest in the spirit of a Loyola. It is even hard to believe how he could have passed his theological examinations in fundamental dogmatics. He does not sink into obscurity, he positively searches for it. His deepest desire is for a life with only the simplest demands of human responsibilities — a *vita minima*. The Kar affords the priest the kind of shelter that the garden wing had offered him, the people there are undemanding and do not pose a challenge that he cannot meet. The poor parish and the desolate region also meet his need for self-castigation and at the same time offer him the means to prove himself worthy. One even wonders whether he is trying to atone for the fact that he exists at all. Yet there is also a strange element of self-gratification in his hoarding of money as it facilitates the mortification of the flesh.

There still remains the question of the linen. If the whole logic of his poverty is to strip himself of every kind of material wealth in order to provide money for a new school, why does he not obey the clear injunction of Christ to the rich young man, 'go and sell that thou hast and give to the poor'? The priest is conscious of this sin but unable to remedy it. His words are very carefully chosen, poignant and revealing in their modulation from 'sin', an act of transgression against a divine law, to 'fault', a defect of character, to 'weakness', an inability to resist a particular temptation, ending with the emotive admission 'Es wäre gar zu traurig, wenn ich die Wäsche weggeben müßte' (p.92), clearly indicating that his feelings and emotions have got the better of his conscience, his religious vows and his rational self, that in the daily struggle to combat them, he is always the loser. Suddenly his way of life, which to the surveyor seemed merely eccentric, takes on another meaning. The vicious circle the poor priest is caught in stands revealed. Yet even the attentive reader who realises that no fellow priest would absolve the priest feels at a loss to define what the white linen could really mean for the priest and stands baffled by the mystery.

The strange fact in all this welter of conjecture is that we welcome the turn given by the story that the sole channel of expression of all these complex feelings is through the obsession with white linen and shining silver. It is not so much the things themselves — though we cannot help wondering about the actual sensual delight of the caressing touch of the soft shirts — as the persistence in retaining them in the face of both his material poverty and his deep feeling of guilt, which is deeper than his feeling of shame.

Stifter's purpose and control in giving this life-story are admirably clear. While, on the one hand, he appears to be gratifying our commonplace interests in what made the hero 'tick' and supplying the surveyor with the sort of knowledge he would like to hear, we hear a quite different voice emerging: that of a human soul which knows its own weakness and yet feels inextricably guilty. Lest one should be tempted in this situation simply to follow the surveyor's lead in assuming one now knows everything there is to know, Stifter immediately after the account proceeds to debunk the surveyor's standing as a guide even further. The surveyor fulfils to the letter the expectations the priest had of him as an executor of his will, but he fails him as a friend. He fails very much in the way that we must admit is the norm in such circumstances. He visits the priest once more in the Kar, because his work takes him into the neighbourhood. After that, his professional and personal obligations take over. Even when he receives a letter telling him of the priest's illness, and containing the poignant phrase 'Wenn er es wüßte, daß ich krank bin' (p.95), he cannot find the time to visit him. Yet, as usual in such circumstances, the obstacles can be removed when it comes to going to the priest's funeral and the opening of his will. Again, there is no authorial comment. The surveyor's own words reveal and condemn. Stifter makes him sound complacent in the way he describes how he too contributed to the success of the priest's modest plan, how he bought the fine linen and the crucifix which, the reader remembers, once caught his eye as a beautiful piece of medieval carving.

But while from the surveyor's point of view Stifter lets the story come to its happy ending, he once more brings back to the consciousness of the attentive reader the many unanswered questions he is left with, and the feeling of the essential ambiguities of the whole story. They find their symbolic and ironic expression in the surveyor's naive description of the clothes the priest's body is dressed in for his modest lying-in-state. 'Man legte ihm das Schönste seiner Wäsche an. Dann zog man ihm sein fadenscheiniges Kleid an und über das Kleid den Priesterchorrock. So wurde er auf der Bahre ausgestellt' (p.97). The puzzled reader is forced to ask himself what Stifter is driving at by this carefully structured passage. Is he once again simply showing up the obtuseness of the surveyor who is immune to the irony of his own observations, or is he suggesting that the priest is taking his secret to the grave, or is he going much further, hinting darkly at the spectre of eternal damnation for the humble priest who fought so hard?

What makes this story so impressive and fascinating is that the priest's behaviour with his finery draws together so many thoughts about what really moves men in the depths of their being, of a life that goes on well below the surface, that we have to call this central point of the story an inexhaustible mystery. The beautiful soft linen, the furtive gesture hiding it, become a real symbol for man's position as a fly in a spider's web of complicated, contradictory and complementary feelings and emotions. But Stifter wants us to understand that the purposefulness with which the priest sets up and pursues a task that gives meaning to his life is of paramount importance. It helps him to accept himself, the burden of his past and all that cannot be changed.

The idea of creating the figure of the narrator and of lending him a clearly discernible personality, moulded by his work and social standing, with an easily definable attitude to life, gave Stifter a great amount of artistic freedom. He could use him to give his tale a firm perspective, but one which he could undermine at will. He could lull his reader into what seemed, on the surface, safe assumptions about the meaning and purpose of the story, only to lead him to realise that what he had taken for the full extent of the meaning was dangerously restricted by the narrator's subjective point of view and personal limitations. Because he fashioned the narrator into a normal, healthy, successful man, he could, in juxtaposing him with the priest, lay bare his shortcomings and criticise the whole of that society of which he was a plausible representative and to which many of his own readers belonged. By showing the surveyor in an ironic light he could challenge that reader to draw on his own finer and deeper resources of understanding and perception, to allow his imagination full rein and to develop a finer susceptibility than that of the well-meaning, observant but ultimately narrow surveyor. Stifter was thus able to educate his reader in stages, without forcing the issue or making this too obvious. In doing this Stifter could also act out his own inner longing to be a writer with a mission, to contribute his mite towards a more enlightened, more morally refined society that would be able to appreciate the hidden worth of an individual. By the same token this bold design also allowed him to be naturally secretive. He had the perfect tool to keep an otherwise plain tale tantalisingly mysterious. This use of the surveyor convinces me that Stifter here found a narrative device which served as a means of dispensing himself as man and as artist from having to face up squarely to the disturbing emotions, bordering on the sinister and pathological, which the story strongly suggests but never brings out into the open.

To any reader who may now be inclined to accept the claim made for this story in my opening sentences I would have to concede that there is a great shift of emphasis in passing from Shakespeare's celebration of man to Stifter's. We come nearer to our author if, as we shut the book, we recall the Psalmist's exclamation, 'I will praise Thee, for I am fearfully and wonderfully made'.

5. 'Turmalin'

While Stifter allows *Kalkstein* to end on a note of reconciliation
— there is after all the new school in the Kar as a tangible proof
that the priest had managed to wring some kind of good result
from his deep sense of sin, and in so doing inspired others to step
from their narrow circle of selfish preoccupations — no such
redeeming gesture is proffered in *Turmalin*. The life of the
eccentric Rentherr begins in the anonymity of the big city and is
swallowed up by it without trace in the end. Unlike the poor
priest the Rentherr is incapable, by constitution as much as by
inclination, one feels, of finding within himself any kind of
integrity, moral or intellectual. He lets himself drift in selfish
abandonment to grief and thoughts of revenge, dragging his
daughter with him. While Herder could say that the adversities
of life sharpened man's intelligence and enabled him to emerge
from his cave, we have here the retrograde process, the clouding
of reason, the flight to caves, the life in the basement, the only
source of light obscured by the dirt and refuse of the street. We
can only conjecture what pessimistic thoughts made Stifter write
this frustration of the great hopes of the Enlightenment.

Turmalin is a savage tale of the Swiftian kind that forces us to
think more of what must have happened to the author than to
grieve over the sad fates of the chief personages in the story.
This impression of savagery is heightened if we bring in the fact
that as late as 1852 Stifter published, *Der Pförtner im
Herrenhause*, a story containing the very same events, which
glorifies practical morality according to the 'sanfte Gesetz' and
concludes with Stifter's favourite theme of the grandeur of the
moral feelings of insignificant people:

> Die größte Begabung, der höchste Glanz des Geistes, der
> die Menschen in Staunen setzt, ist ein Sandkorn — ja ist
> nichts — gegen die tiefe Liebe und die Reinheit des

Gemüthes. Welche Größe lag in den unscheinbaren
Menschen ... welches Unmaß von Liebe lag in ihnen ...
(Jf., p.133).

Der Pförtner im Herrenhause is a feeble tale because the only
solid part is a segment from the life of a female narrator who
exhibits all the practical morality of a comfortable bourgeois
'do-gooder' with a total incapacity to give meaning to the odd
events she finds herself mixed up in. The great love Stifter refers
to has no more existence than details which might appear in a
newspaper account of the adultery and unexplained disappearance of a lower-middle-class couple from their previous
address.

   We can only guess at what terrible experiences Stifter must have
undergone to cause him, so soon after writing this simple, pathetic
little story, to give it such a sinister turn that it reads like a
particular illustration of the ominous last paragraph of the
Vorrede, in which, as we saw, Stifter traced the moral decline and
utter dissolution of a once admirable civilisation, and referred
darkly to his 'eben entwickelten Ansichten und die Erlebnisse
der letztvergangenen Jahre' (p.12). For although among the
causes of this decline he listed 'in ihrer Kunst wird das Einseitige
geschildert' (p.12), nothing in that *Vorrede* could prepare us for
the sickened horror with which Stifter contemplates the
desecration of art in the hands of the perverted dilettante who
has no other business in life than to play about with *objets d'art*,
and to cultivate his aesthetic sensibility. And more terrible than
the moral consequences of such behaviour is the revelation that
the figure of love of the first version turns into a picture of lovelessness and total alienation from what makes human life
worthy and precious. Whatever these experiences were, the main
change brought about in the final version is to alter the whole
balance of the story and to concentrate our attention on the
initial state of the married couple and their baby before their
lives are broken up by the wife's adultery and disappearance.
Through all the weird and improbable changes in the fortunes of
father and child we are constantly forced back to see whether we
can discover the causal chain of these bizarre effects in the

father's inner nature and initial choice of life.

The admirer of Dickens's novels of London life will note several similarities between the treatment of the English metropolis and the political centre of the Austrian Empire. It is not merely the fascination with the sheer variety and oddity of its streets and squares, its boulevards and its back alleys, but also with the urban efficiency of its modern administration. Much of the later history of the missing Viennese couple gains its mystery from a contrast between the city's efficient modern bureaucracy which 'keeps tabs' on every citizen, preserves property rights, sees to the coroner's inquests and the burials of untraceable vagrants, and, on the other hand, the ease with which an individual can slip through the net, and be lost to public view and to public memory. No connected history can be provided of such people, and therefore we marvel the more over the unknown *real* chain which must have been forged between the initial moment of the couple's public existence and the next public event, the findings of an inquest over an unidentified corpse. Another Dickensian trait which gives colour to the story is the provision of evidence of what could be seen in all the great European capitals during these years of the mid-nineteenth century, of the rapid changes in the visible shell of the city. Old landmarks were ruthlessly demolished to make way for modern traffic, new offices and municipal buildings changed the appearance of the principal quarters. Only here and there the decayed ruins of once splendid houses still lingered on as slum haunts to remind the thoughtful observer of the impermanence even of an eternal city like Rome with her thousand years of history behind her.

Although we can only conjecture what made Stifter change a chance event into something nearer a tragedy, nothing prevents us saluting the art in the pages which were most heavily worked over dealing with the material setting in which the couple lived a life which might have run its course as a typical *rentier* existence of cultivated, well-to-do people with no great sense of purpose in all their doings. If we paid no special attention to the rhythms and the syntax of Stifter's prose in these descriptions, we might think they resembled the happy knack of Balzac or Dickens in piling up picturesque accounts of the bric-a-brac with which the houses of the bourgeois in this period were cluttered. But when we note how carefully each item in the Rentherr's 'Heldenstube' is made to stand out separately, it may come over us that here, as in the other tales, every detail is loaded with Stifter's unspoken commentary. We might say that it is simultaneously a Dutch still-life or interior painting and an emblem or a forest of symbols. Stifter allows himself only one explicit comment, 'wunderlich', to tell us that with the Rentherr we are dealing with a 'Mensch, wie in solchen großen Städten verschiedene Arten von Menschen wohnen und sich mit den verschiedensten Dingen beschäftigen' (p.103).

Before the full implications of these passages dawn on us, we might think that Stifter is merely laughing at the eager 'culture-vulture' who provides his well-upholstered couches with castors to permit them to flit more easily to the most advantageous viewpoints for enjoying his many *objets d'art*. And we might still linger with the thought that Stifter is presenting not only the comic but also the grotesque aspects of this queer cult of art and its objects. The graver thoughts are slow to appear. If everything we see tells us that the dilettante has no inner centre, no firm inner principle, we do not at once conclude that he is therefore doomed to insanity and permanent exclusion from normal society.

If we hesitate to read more into Stifter's account of the man's study and studio, we are nevertheless prepared, when we come to the parallel picture of his wife's apartment, for the unspeakable horrors that unfold before us. A single passage will put the evidence in a nutshell:

> In der Nähe dieses Bettes stand auf einem Gestelle ein vergoldeter Engel, welcher die Flügel um die Schultern zusammengefaltet hielt, mit der einen Hand sich stützte, die andere aber sanft ausstreckte, und mit den Fingern die Spitze eines weißen Vorhanges hielt, der in reichen Falten in der Gestalt eines Zeltes auseinander- und niederging. Unter diesem Zelte stand auf einem Tische ein feiner Korb, in dem Korbe war ein weißes Bettchen, und in dem

Bettchen war das Kind der beiden Eheleute, das Mädchen, bei dem sie öfter standen und die winzigen roten Lippen und die rosigen Wangen und die geschlossenen Äuglein betrachteten. Zu Schlusse war noch ein sehr schön gemaltes großes Bild in dem Zimmer, die heilige Mutter mit dem Kinde vorstellend. Es war mit einer Faltung von dunkelm Sammet umgeben (p.106).

Stifter, I take it, is ordering us to read between the lines and to declare that just as there was no real, live baby in the room, so there was no presence of the Blessed Virgin. We have been in a museum of stuffed objects. (It is hard to believe that the two puppets could between them have produced even a semblance of a human child.)

But if we go so far as this, we have to declare that the tale is *not* a tragedy. Stifter no doubt felt the horror of such degenerate specimens coming to stand for contemporary culture, but he could not himself have constructed the chain whose links are carefully hidden from us by the want of news about the man and his daughter. Stifter at his best always knows perfectly well what he withholds and leaves us to find. Henry James once asserted that he could stand a stiff examination on the motives and inner thoughts of one of his personages; and similarly Stifter, I feel sure, had followed and 'miterlebt' every moment of the poor priest in *Kalkstein*, from his first breath to his last. We can see in what sense Stifter was ignorant in *Turmalin* if we ask, where does his man come into contact with the real? The adulterer is a straw figure, a walking formula for a well-known type of second-rate but popular actor. His success with the wife is wholly off-stage, because Stifter had no material to back up what would have been the powerfully tragic conviction which caused the husband to tell his wife, 'sie habe an Dall fallen müssen' (p.109). This is even weaker than the earlier version, where we at least find a vague reference to necessity: 'es sei das schon alles so in der Nothwendigkeit gewesen, daß es gekommen sei' (Jf., p.117).

Stifter would have had to re-write the whole second part to make the story a tragic whole. The slight changes do not alter the fact that once again we have a happening, a series of happenings. If it *was* so, we do not see the necessity. We cannot say that everything had to be so.

The tale does, however, exhibit one kind of connection: there is a running theme with several nicely varied examples planted out at intervals throughout the pages. This is the theme which begins so powerfully when we meet the Rentherr and to a less powerful degree when we find that Dall is also one of the Devil's disciples perverting art to unworthy ends. A clue that might be exploited to test this hypothesis may be found if we note what a crude link Professor Andorf is in the earlier version of the tale, a clumsy device to connect the female 'do-gooder' to the 'Perronsche' mansion. In *Turmalin* Stifter goes out of his way to describe him first as a good man, a morally worthy and cultivated amateur of the arts; '... er hatte ein warmes empfindendes Herz und war für alles Gute und Schöne empfänglich' (p.118). A striking contrast, one might think, to Dall and the Rentherr. Yet Stifter again goes out of his way to characterise him as one who, instead of developing his creative gifts, devoted his talents to savouring and studying 'das allmähliche Versinken, Vergehen, Verkommen' (p.119) of the old house that was crumbling away before his eyes. This is such a gratuitous addition to the plot that we may legitimately suspect that the passage was aimed allegorically at one set of Stifter's *bêtes noires*, uncreative aesthetic exquisites.

A similar conclusion must be drawn, I would say, from Stifter's failure to remedy the weakest feature of his story, the history of the girl's underground education. A critic worth his salt must begin as a doubting Thomas, and challenge his author with 'show me! show me!'. Has anyone been able to believe that Stifter could have transcribed a single sentence of the 'Schriftdeutsch' spoken by the girl, or a paragraph from one of her many 'Dichtungen'? Are we to suppose that the father could bring about such effects if he himself was really off his head, had less than six hours a day for oral instruction, and understood the process of education so little, was so ignorant of Pestalozzi or Rousseau (to say nothing of the wise grandfather in *Granit*) as to propose such essay topics as he did to a girl who had no idea of life or death and knew mankind only between the ankle and the knee? We must all have wondered how Miranda got such a fine education, but Prospero was not mad and was a magician!

I argue from this failure to overcome our scepticism that Stifter was not entering into his story as an artist but was blowing off steam about the abuse of education in the literate classes. Yet if these lines are a satire:

> Ich nahm mir nun, wenn ich Zeit hatte, die Mühe, den größten Teil dieser Papiere zu durchlesen. Was soll ich davon sagen? Ich würde sie Dichtungen nennen, wenn Gedanken in ihnen gewesen wären, oder wenn man Grund, Ursprung und Verlauf des Ausgesprochenen hätte enträtseln können. Von einem Verständnisse, was Tod, was Umirren in der Welt und sich aus Verzweiflung das Leben nehmen heiße, war keine Spur vorhanden, und doch war dieses alles der trübselige Inhalt der Ausarbeitungen. Der Ausdruck war klar und bündig, der Satzbau richtig und gut, und die Worte, obwohl sinnlos, waren erhaben (p.136),

they could not reach and hurt those whom the cap fitted.

An even greater failure of the close is the let-down for the 'sanfte Gesetz'. What happens when the glowing lines quoted earlier from *Der Pförtner* about the elevating power of great love in humble hearts can no longer be applied? The answer is clear: we descend from religious poetry and fairy magic to a prose level, where it is no insult to the worthy 'do-gooder' to give her the name. The changes Stifter made for *Turmalin* while preserving her as an agent of practical morality, effectively prevent her becoming in any way a ministering angel. It is very sad to see how many miles we travel from Dostoievsky or Dickens or Stifter himself in more confident days, when the girl with hydrocephalus is treated merely as a case for social welfare, and when we find her being economically integrated into society once she comes into the very much diminished remains of her father's wealth, and is then promptly dropped from the do-gooder's busy life. There is no mention of her in the epilogue which recalls Dall. She is lost in the anonymity of the modern metropolis.

We have therefore every reason to think of the author rather than the tale, who has left the irredeemable unredeemed and given the last words to dust, transience and oblivion. I think we have to posit a sudden bitterness welling up after *Der Pförtner*, which tempted Stifter into recording his real misgivings about the world he found himself in after 1848. For many of the letters he wrote at this time reiterate the theme of his disappointment, and, above all, his disgust with the role being played by the educated classes, on whose sense of moderation he had set such high hopes. *Turmalin* seems to spring straight from the kind of outburst we find in a letter of 6 March 1849:

> Das war ein fürchterliches Jahr! Ich habe mich in Bezug der Dinge, die da kommen werden, keinen Augenblik getäuscht, als ich nur einmal von der Haupttäuschung frei war, nehmlich von der, *von unsern sogenannten gebildeten Leuten etwas zu halten* ... Ich habe diesen Sommer durch so vieles Schlechte, Freche, Unmenschliche und Dumme, das sich dreist machte, und für Höchstes ausgab, *unsäglich* gelitten. Was in mir groß, gut, schön, und vernünftig war, empörte sich, selbst *Tod* ist süßer, als solch ein Leben, wo Sitte Heiligkeit Kunst Göttliches nichts mehr ist ...

6. 'Katzensilber'

In Stifter's originally planned arrangement of the stories *Katzensilber* would have immediately followed *Turmalin*. Indeed, in spite of its totally different subject matter, setting and narrative mode, it seems to be imbued with a similarly pessimistic disgust with the well-to-do and educated — this time the newly-risen landowners — and their false scale of values. The melancholy mood that pervades it seems to express the same kind of resignation that we find in a letter of 8 November 1851: 'Meine theure Freundin, die mich so oft erfreut getröstet geliebt hat, die Natur, auch diese hat ihr Antlitz geändert, seit man weiß, daß Menschen in ihr herum gehen, die so sind, wie sie eben sind.'

Katzensilber is a strange, elusive story, as strange and elusive as the brown girl herself. In structure it is the simplest of the tales in the *Bunte Steine*: it has no framework, no flashback, no intricate time-sequences, no long and ponderous theoretical introduction. The reason why no such elaborations are required is clear. The given elements of the scene, human and geographical, are so richly suggestive in their own right that we can pass from the simple surface of children's pleasures to the ultimate reaches of the human spirit with such ease and speed that no commentator or stage-director is needed to inform us where at each moment we stand. *Katzensilber* has some of the felicity of Shakespeare's inspired use of the crassly human play-actors in the fairies' 'wood near Athens' of his *A Midsummer Night's Dream*, where nobody is surprised to find the fairies intervening in human affairs and humans mixed up in fairies' quarrels. But Stifter has further advantages denied to Shakespeare, in that his frontiers are more primitive, much closer to those confronting the first men, whose outer lives were at the mercy of natural disasters and carnivorous animals, men whose own nature was unknown to them and in consequence their imagination was peopled by terrible demons not to be safely located in dreams or companioning them in lonely places, and therefore 'projected' into nature myths. Although, as will appear, Stifter manipulated his given elements in such a way as to bring into our consciousness the special terrors in the souls of men of his own day, yet many of those elements both in the natural world and in the fairy-stories he alludes to are, in the natural history of man, centuries older than Shakespeare's, for whom the excursions beyond the civilised matter-of-fact have all the pleasures of a witty game. For Stifter the frontiers separating the kingdoms of the tame and the wild are full of peril for those who fail to observe the correct behaviour to be used when they pass from one realm to the other. Much of the dramatic quality of the tale arises from the elusive transitions between scenes of calm and scenes of peril, between moments when everything is grossly palpable, and others when nothing is tangible.

Long before T.S. Eliot introduced the term 'objective correlative', Stifter found the perfect introduction to his chosen theme in the opening pages containing the detailed description of the enlightened, perceptive way in which the owner of the estate looks after his property, tries to understand the particular character of the countryside he lives in and to exploit and adapt to his own profit the possibilities in the natural environment. We learn how he cultivates fruits, vegetables and flowers, with what special care and labour he has carved a kind of garden out of the wild land surrounding the farm. Even in this leisurely description of a peaceful, normal existence, we cannot forget the close proximity of the civilised and the wild:

> Um das Haus liegen, wie es in jenem Lande immer vorkömmt, in nähern und fernern Kreisen Hügel, die mit Feldern und Wiesen bedeckt sind, manches Bauernhaus, manchen Meierhof zeigen, und auf dem Gipfel jedesmal den Wald tragen, der wie nach einem verabredeten Gesetz alle Gipfel jenes hügligen Landes besetzt. Zwischen den Hügeln, die oft, ohne daß man es ahnt, in steile Schluchten abfallen, gehen Bäche, ja zuweilen Gießbäche, über welche Stege und in abgelegenen Teilen gar nur Baumstämme

führen. Regelmäßige Brücken haben nur die Fahrwege, wo
sie über einen solchen Bach gehen müssen. Das ganze Land
geht gegen Mitternacht immer mehr empor, bis die
größeren düsteren weitgedehnten Wälder kommen, die den
Beginn der böhmischen Länder bezeichnen. Gegen Mittag
sieht man die freundliche blaue Kette der Hochgebirge an
dem Himmel dahinstreichen (p.186).

In this beautiful passage we have set out before us all the
varied aspects of the landscape from the 'freundlich' to the
'groß', 'düster', and 'weitgedehnt' of the vast Bohemian forests
which form the arena in which all the events in the story have
their locus. This is the nature the children traverse on all their
repeated excursions to the woods: they leave the warm, sunlit
region of their garden with its fruit trees, flowers and smooth
lawns for the gloomy woods and from there climb the grassy
mountain slopes until they finally come to the Nußberg. The
external natural scene has an interior mirror: while the children
rest in 'der weiten glänzenden Luft' (p.192), they listen to the
mysterious legends told by the grandmother of spirits and
hobgoblins who inhabit these regions.

The 'Braune Mädchen' emerges straight from this unknown
sphere of nature, 'als ... sie wieder einmal auf dem hohen
Nußberge an der dicken veralteten Haselwurzel saßen, kam aus
dem Gebüsche ein fremdes braunes Kind heraus' (p.197), and
she mysteriously disappears back into it 'daß man die Zweige
sich rühren sah' (p.197). Throughout the story she remains both
the 'braune', that is, the nut-brown maid of the folk ballad, and
the 'fremde Mädchen', an alien, mysterious, unidentifiable
stranger. The farmer searching for her human aspect, her family
and homeland, is led further and further away and higher into
the mountain regions. Although many of the peasants,
cottagers, charcoal-burners and woodcutters to whom he
describes the girl claim to have seen her, nobody knows where
she comes from.

One principal object of the story is to heighten the contrast
between the vast threatening area and the little peaceful oasis
where all is safe. A second object is to show the failure of the

genteel folk to make contact with or to comprehend the utter difference. Stifter goes out of his way to make us uneasy with his repetitious accounts of the monotonous similarity of the children's 'nature walks'. The total incongruity of the two worlds comes over us when Stifter twice supplies a detailed list of what the children wore on these walks from the white pantaloons peeping from underneath their skirts to the little bags hanging from their shoulders. The absence of childish exuberance on these expeditions is uncanny. The children hardly ever skip or run. The predominant verb 'gingen' is repeated over and over again. What a contrast with the 'springen', 'eilen' and 'laufen' used to describe the movements of the brown girl! The whole attempt by the children to get in touch with the spirit of the natural world is shown to be futile. They might just as well be taking a constitutional round the well laid out gravel paths of a civic park. An even crasser example is the father's idea to build a little Wendy house on the 'Nußberg' with its painted posies of flowers in the four corners of the room, its pretty furniture, where the grandmother lays out all the paraphernalia of an over-civilised lifestyle with its white, starched linen, silver spoons, little napkins, silver ladle, milk, honey and white rolls.

The extent to which the civilised world is threatened both from without and within is laid bare by the irruption of the elemental forces of the hailstorm and the fire. They both bring to the surface and expose what had lain hidden, that which was amiss in the ordered world of genteel society. Here we must distinguish sharply two quite different areas of failure. One concerns ignorance or incompetence in dealing with Nature in her fiercer aspects. The other is an ugly streak of heartlessness and selfishness in the adults, which is only faintly echoed in the behaviour of the children. It is not a moral fault in the grandmother but merely an exposure of her total alienation from nature when she, who had all along prided herself on her superior knowledge of the countryside, its climate and folklore, cannot read the signs of the oncoming storm and fails to find the submerged bridge over the flooded stream. It is, however, a disagreeable trait of heartlessness in the old woman, as Stifter himself stresses in his narrative, that she cares more to secure her own shelter during the storm than to look after the protection of the brown girl. But it is a monstrous fault in both mother and grandmother to forget a child, one of only three, in a burning house, a fault which becomes more damning when we learn the cause. While the mother, when she discovers the fire, immediately runs to a desk to save a casket of valuables and rushes out of the house with the children 'ohne zu achten, ob sie zwei oder drei seien' (p.231), the grandmother is guilty of an equally serious offence when in her anxiety to protect the family's property from thieves she locks a door, thus condemning the boy to death in the fire. Both women, of course, never consciously intend such a fate for the child but endanger his life in their preponderant concern for the material objects of their wealth.

Although nothing that has so far emerged casts doubt on Stifter's own belief in the possibility of a world of spiritual activity inherent in the old legends and stories, we may question the strength of the grandmother's adherence to the traditional beliefs. The children at any rate are so far from awe or wonder that when she tells them tales of strange men in the past coming to the streams to pan for gold and find pearls in the shells, their instant reaction is that of a scientific sceptic:

> Für sich allein standen die Kinder gerne am Bache, wo er sanft fließt und allerlei krause Linien zieht, und blickten auf den Sand, der wohl wie Gold war, wenn die Sonne durch das Wasser auf ihn schien, und der glänzende Blättchen und Körner zeigte. Wenn sie aber mit einem Schäufelchen Sand herausholten und gut wuschen und schwemmten, so waren die Blättchen Katzensilber, und die Körner waren schneeweiße Stückchen von Kiesel. Muscheln waren wenige zu sehen, und wenn sie eine fanden, so war sie im Innern glatt, und es war keine Perle darin (p.196).

It seems to me that the children's effortless deflation of magic and their turning away from the implicit religion in the strange tales told about the mysteries of nature in the mountain regions

are more significant than all the other detailed examples Stifter
assembles in this story to illustrate the family's alienation from
the essential forces of nature and ultimately of life as a whole.
So much so, indeed, that Stifter here seems to be undermining
his own carefully built up atmosphere of the numinous, and to
be making nonsense of the many stylistic and structural features
that he borrowed from the traditional folk-tale. We are forced
to question the original supposition about Stifter's intention to
set up a contrast between the wild and the tame, between the
mysterious girl who comes and goes in the forest and the family
who with such care and circumspection wrest cultivated land
from the wilderness.

   To find an answer we have to turn to the point at the end of
the story where Stifter, who had been keeping the nature and
identity of the brown girl a secret, finally identifies her with a
figure in a well-known legend. Her whole behaviour, her con-
vulsive weeping, her very words, 'Sture Mure ist tot, und der
hohe Felsen ist tot' (p.241), the way she runs up the sandy slopes
to the wilderness beyond, never to be seen again, force us to see
her at last as a figure in one of the grandmother's tales, where a
mysterious message is delivered about the death of an unknown
person. For her words clearly echo those in the folk-tale: 'Jochträger, Jochträger, sag der Sture Mure, die Rauh-Rinde sei tot'
(p.189). The two-fold repetition of this haunting message now
caught up with the girl's own parting words 'opens the moral' as
Pope would say, of the whole story, and reminds us of the most
potent of all the legends which record the last words of a nature
power to an unbelieving human world.

   Stifter carries us back through the centuries to a legend
recorded by Plutarch.[11] In the reign of Tiberius, the pilot,
Thamus, while sailing by the island of Paxi, heard a mighty
voice proclaiming, 'Great Pan is dead'. Pan was thought to be a
rustic god, a wood-spirit conceived in the form of a goat,
traversing the tops of mountains and bringing fertility to the
flocks. When it was noticed by Christians that this voice had
spoken at the time of the birth or the crucifixion of Christ, the

---

11 Plutarch, *De orac. defectu*, 17. Cf. Lutz Röhrich, *Sage* (Stuttgart, Metzler, 1966), pp.2, 19, 28f., 41, 66.

incident was thought to mark the end of the old world and the beginning of the new. Through the lesser deities associated with Pan, legends of this message passed into the folklore of Europe, and fathered a host of figures of local interest. Among them are spirits who come and serve humans for a time only to disappear for ever from human ken when they hear the message that 'Stutzi-Mutzi', 'Rohrinde', or any other local deity who had taken the place of Pan, has died.[12]

Stifter cannot have intended his brown girl's words to be totally incomprehensible. He must have expected that his cultivated readers, if they had not read Plutarch's essay on the silence of the oracles, to have either heard in oral tradition or to have read in one or other of the recently published collections of Austrian folk-tales stories similar to that of Sture Mure, for this was a wonderful stroke which enlarges Stifter's story of one family to embrace the whole of our speculation about the relation of the natural to the supernatural.[13]

Yet when we compare Stifter's portrayal of the brown girl with that of any dryads as they appear in the local legends he drew on, we realise how lacking she is in the vigorous, awe-inspiring, menacing aspects of a true leprechaun. Stifter never allows her to display truly magical powers in her sudden appearances in moments of danger; her acts of bravery are always just plausible enough to be natural. Nowhere does he endow her with the strength of a giantess or the vitality of the young dryad, a 'Rutschi-Fenka-Meiggi', who aroused general amazement by her feats of dancing. Although she saves Sigismund three times, and a special bond is formed between them, she never claims him for her own, either dead or alive. In

[12] That this myth had occurred to Stifter was noted by Anton Avanzin, 'Die sagenmäßige Grundlage von Stifters *Katzensilber*', *Österreichische Zeitschrift für Volkskunde* 15 (1964), 274-76; *Leopold Schmidt*, 'Volkskundliche Betrachtungen an den Werken Adalbert Stifters', *Adalbert-Stifter-Almanach für 1953*, pp.87-108; Joachim Müller (*32*, p.152). Professor Müller, however, saw no special significance for *Katzensilber*, nor did I in my article (*31*).

[13] Cf. for example: Franz Joseph Vonbun, *Die Sagen Vorarlbergs mit Beiträgen aus Liechtenstein*, (Innsbruck, 1847, 2nd ed. 1850); Johann Nep. R. von Alpenburg, *Mythen und Sagen Tirols* (Innsbruck, 1857) and *Deutsche Alpensagen* (Wien, 1861); Ignaz V. Zingerle, *Sagen aus Tirol* (Innsbruck, 2nd ed., 1891), all of which contain versions of this myth, and some in language strikingly similar to Stifter's.

his descriptions of nature, Stifter conjures up the darkness of the forests, the steep valleys and hidden torrents, and when evoking the force of hailstorms and fire he unleashes the full power of the elements, but there is nothing in the girl which corresponds to all this. Indeed, to claim her as a symbol of anything so grand as Nature would be to strip her of much of her gentle, sad appeal.

Stifter seems unable to bridge this difficulty. There is no doubt that he was trying in *Katzensilber* to express a feeling, an intuitive unease, that modern society, however civilised and well intentioned, is for ever separated and alienated from the natural. Modern man may take a sentimental interest in natural beauties but cannot comprehend and come to terms with its mysteries. It is therefore the most frightening, almost nihilistic aspect of the tale that its main characters are unconscious of all this, learn nothing, and the only standards they know are those that apply to their own conditions. Yet, if one looks at Stifter's anaemic portrayal of his brown girl, one must sadly conclude that, although he knew all this, he himself had lost the inner conviction to counter this modern development by creating a vital symbol of the alternative.

It may be for this reason that he was forced to borrow, more than in his other stories, from literary conventions. The fairy-tales are one example, Goethe's Mignon is another. There were times when Stifter thought of himself as upholding part of Goethe's heritage. While there certainly is a link, however tenuous, uniting the best of Stifter's writing and his ideas on enlightened humanism with those of Goethe after his Italian journey, a comparison of the brown girl and Mignon reveals the gulf that separates them. Mignon is always fully real, she is more real than all the other characters in *Wilhelm Meister*. The power to create such a figure comes from the author's passionate conviction that there really was a purer form of existence, nearer the source of life, and we know it is so from Mignon's ability to suffer. She is not a pathetic figure such as the brown girl at times appears, but is truly tragic. And therein lies the whole difference between the two authors. Consequently, it is not the brown girl we feel sorry for but the author, whose creative gift seems to have been sapped by an all-pervading pessimism, perhaps by a loss of his own belief that if man can learn at all, it is from the unchanging laws of nature, that by opening his heart and his mind to the miraculous beauty of nature, he can be enabled to go on believing in something higher, more harmonious than himself.

But with such a complicated figure as Stifter, we should be wary of putting forward such a simple explanation. His failure to convert the brown girl into a valid symbol of the spiritual forces in nature may be due to a general literary difficulty. It may simply be that all that comprises tragedy was just too much for him. He clearly wished to express the pain and terror in human existence and the reality of a force outside ourselves that passes our rational comprehension, but *Katzensilber* gives the impression that in every sense of the term Stifter was 'covering up'. Though he may not have understood the full import of what he was saying, I think he told the truth in a letter he wrote on 31 March 1853 to an admirer of the story when he said, 'Ich hielt das Kazensilber für das beste und zarteste Stük, und das unausgesprochene Gefühl des braunen Mädchens, als sie die Kinder suchte und endlich wieder fliehen mußte, für das wehmüthigste, daher ich mich bestimmt fühlte, das arme Kind mit der größten Schonung und seine Lage mit dem liebevollsten Schleier zu behandeln'.

7. 'Bergmilch'

Whereas in all the other tales, however many the difficulties and weaknesses they may contain, the reader has to salute the masterly touches of art, the wonderful control of apparently irrelevant details which are painstakingly woven together to concentrate his mind on the point of the tale, the very opposite seems to be the truth in *Bergmilch*. Instead of a design we have a disjointed jumble of unrelated incidents. As we follow through the story, we find ourselves looking now one way, now another, and when we look back on completing it, we cannot see a central thread, we cannot discover by any means how the different parts could be described as parts of a whole. For example, the first two pages contain a disquisition on several forms of fortifying castles through the ages. There is a long section, the only point of which seems to be to explain how a collection of eccentrics could settle down into a harmonious household in which all class differences were forgotten. Several other parts are clearly the relics, largely unaltered, of a sentimental tale, first published in 1843 as *Die Wirkungen eines weißen Mantels*. Here the point of the anecdote was the difficulty felt by children in distinguishing acts of bravery from acts of prudence in the stress of war. In *Bergmilch* there is no sign of a directing mind, which, by a wonderful use of language, gradually takes control of the reader and leads him into a world which only Stifter could have created. We become dimly aware of fumbling attempts made by Stifter to tackle the problem of conquering the instincts which lead men into fighting wars and that of discovering a just equilibrium of power between the rival social classes. It would have been better for his reputation if the second volume of *Bunte Steine* had appeared one story short. Nothing more underlines the extent to which chaos overcame Stifter's mind when he rewrote this story than the solemn attempts by critics to find a unifying meaning for the whole of *Bergmilch*, such as that the cranky, eccentric trio could be regarded as emblematic of total unison — the family circle as representing the undivided family of man, or that the eventual marriage of Lulu to the young reckless officer and the production of two children is for Stifter an allegory of a morally rejuvenated future society, or that the resolution of conflict in this family is Stifter's way of pointing to the ideal of peace among nations. Here, in my view, these would-be-unifying critics are not taking the will for the deed so much as inventing the will itself and fathering it upon Stifter. The story bears all the marks of hurried work and shows that Stifter justly assessed the particular needs of his narrative gift when he wrote to his publisher, pleading for more time, 'Ich schreibe durchschnittlich täglich fünf Seiten ... rein, aber oft kann man über Stellen nicht weg, Sie glauben nicht, wie ich mich abquäle, ich weiß das Höhere, und es gestaltet sich nicht, nur die völlige Poesielosigkeit arbeitet ganz leicht weg, und bringt Massen zu Tage, gerade die *lezte Ausfeile* ist das feinste, und bedingt die Schönheit allein' (3 February 1852). He might very well have been referring to this story when in his introduction he asked his readers, if they found a piece of glass among the coloured stones, to think as he did when picking one up in a field: 'es hat doch allerlei Farben und mag bei den Steinen belassen bleiben' (p.15). But to treat it with anything like the seriousness that the other stories call for is to belittle their merit.

The reflection of a growing pessimism can be detected in the collection, especially if we consider the originally planned arrangement of the stories. As planned, *Granit*, *Kalkstein*, *Bergkristall* would have formed the first volume. All these stories appeal to the reader's ability and readiness to believe in the working of a providence which could transform even the incredible coincidence in the life of man or his own imperfect efforts into something good, however restricted in range, time and space. In *Turmalin*, which with *Katzensilber* and *Bergmilch* would have made up the second volume, Stifter hardly bothered to transform the coincidence of the woman narrator shaking her duster out of the window at the very moment the Rentherr passes by, into anything resembling the workings of a supernatural power. There is the little bell chiming from the hospital chapel, but that is all. The Rentherr, immured in his eccentricity, knows no greater power to turn to in his grief, for ever condemned to express his sorrows in his lonely flute-playing which lacks any harmony and order and borders on the insane. In *Katzensilber* Stifter takes the loss of faith in the mysterious and miraculous forces in life as his main subject matter. While the old legend of the Death of Pan was thought to mark the end of the old world and its belief in elemental gods, and the coming of the new Christian era, the linking of the brown girl to the 'panisci' is a suggestion that in his own times age-old beliefs were giving way to scepticism. And if we turn to *Bergmilch* it is even clearer that no appeal is made to the belief in the possibility of other motives and powers in the world than those we see in the behaviour of the steward and the officer. Their behaviour is dictated by common sense, practical wisdom, an almost instinctive wish to minimise aggression and preserve life. That is to say, if we were to ask what mission Stifter imagined he was undertaking in writing these two stories, it would be impossible to give the account he himself formulated which brought in the use of the phrase the 'sanfte Gesetz', and so Stifter, I imagine, had to cover up, to paper over, the gap between for instance *Granit* and *Bergmilch*. It is tempting therefore to see in Stifter's final arrangement of the stories a conscious act of dissimulation.

Conclusion

The reader who has followed me this far will have realised that I do not hold with some of the current views on *Bunte Steine*. I do not believe, for example, that the stories are exclusively meant to illustrate the 'sanfte Gesetz' and that their success or failure as works of art can be measured by discovering the extent to which they fulfil its tenets or deviate from them. Nor do I think that other attempts at finding a unifying interpretation for all the tales in the collection can do justice to the varied thoughts on the human condition, the keenly observed details of everyday life, of folklore and natural phenomena that combine to make up the distinctive essence of each individual story, or that they take adequate account of the differences in composition, the many subtle stylistic nuances and carefully varied narrative modes that distinguish one story from another. Indeed, it is when we try to apply such common denominators as 'rescue of children', 'social isolation and integration', 'destruction of order and restoration of harmony' that we become fully aware of how varied the tales really are and the extent to which they elude the possibility of confining them to any one so-called governing idea. For these reasons I would urge the reader of *Bunte Steine* to take Goethe's advice and savour and enjoy each story for its own sake. Stifter himself seems to have been recommending a similar approach when, in his introduction, he likened the collection of tales to the pocketful of stones he had carried home as a boy from the fields and grass verges, and liked to lay out in rows to enjoy and admire the mysterious gleam of their smooth surfaces.

'Stones of various colours' Stifter called the collection, an unassuming name, and one which has greatly irritated the critics who failed to find a clear symbolism relating stone to story. Apart from *Granit* where the stone figures large and significantly in the story itself, there appears to be no clearly

defined relation of this kind. Stifter tells us that he delighted in
collecting pebbles as a child because they kept their beauty
longer than the flowers and grasses which he also carried home.
He dwells lovingly on their many hues, delicate colouring,
sparkle, glitter and gleam. Rather than taking the high *a priori*
road we might turn to this reminiscence for a clue. I believe that
if we follow the child's imagination and allow the stones to
display their colours and their properties, each one seems in fact
to capture the spirit of the tale it is heading. This is especially
true of *Kalkstein* where the stone, the rocks in the valley and the
figure of the parson form an intimately connected unity. But it is
also true of *Bergkristall* where the cold sparkle of the naturally-
grown crystal with its scintillating facets is not so different from
the glitter of a delicately-shaped snowflake or icicle. In
Katzensilber the children sift the shimmering minerals from the
sand at the bottom of the stream in their attempt to get at the
truth of the grandmother's fairy-tales, thus destroying the air of
magic and wonder surrounding them. For *Turmalin* the dark
colouring of the semi-precious stone is again highly significant
of the despairing tenor of that story. The choice of *Bergmilch*
for the last story is perhaps the least apt to kindle the reader's
imagination, the connection seeming only to be the milky-white
colour of the stone and greatcoat, obviously a relic of the
original title *Die Wirkungen eines weißen Mantels*. This,
however, is about all that can be said with assurance of the
appropriate relation of title to tale.

If we are to allow that Stifter was in his own way a man who
considered very deeply, and reflected in maturity on what he
must have been thinking of in his early works, then we might
consider that he chose this title to tell us plainly in what ways the
individual tales are to be taken together. How could the phrase,
'varied, coloured and diverse stones' stand for one thing? What
kind of person could find unity in such disparate objects? Such a
group of stones would never be put in a geological museum
under one class. But there is one place where just this very
collection of stones could have been found: in Stifter's days little
boys had large and capacious pockets and these treasured stones
could go with them everywhere they went. If we asked such a

boy what turned these unconnected items into a collection, I imagine he would have said, 'they all fascinated me. And each one fascinates me more by contrast with the others'. I do not believe that these childish choices were haphazard: in a deep sense the stones chose Stifter as much as he chose them. They are all sources of wonder and mystery that it took *one* mind, Stifter's, and only his, to perceive.

The analogy of the boy's collection would not be helpful if it suggested that the stories at bottom are slight. On the contrary, they are an expression of Stifter's deep concern about his own time. When Stifter came to shape his book, he brought mature and conscious reflection to bear on each individual tale, and this reflection is present in all of them and constitutes the unity in disparity. There is no doubt that in rewriting the versions of the stories Stifter was pursuing a definite policy in changing their often nonchalant, take-it-or-leave-it tone for a strongly-moulded and harmonious combination of elements in which every one plays a part in driving home the meaning of the whole. In rewriting he deliberately diminished the anecdotal, accidental aspects of the stories in favour of more typifying characteristics. The earlier titles had drawn attention to the individual human story each contained. Perhaps the change of these titles to those of stones may be a sign of this wish to emphasise the typical, to make the stories representative of wider issues. This is not to argue that the meaning of each story was something Stifter designed before he wrote and into which he forced the revised story to fit, but that to his mature sight each revealed a subtle and serious reading of an invariable human nature. We thereby gain insight into man as he was and always will be and we measure the success of each story by the predominance of this art over any conceptualising intention he may also have had in rewriting the stories.

In this respect there is a large difference between his very best and his worst story in this collection. Behind this verdict is my conviction that it is general human nature that we are invited to appreciate rather than its peculiarities and oddities. This may sound paradoxical because Stifter deliberately chooses to draw our attention to quaint, eccentric and even bizarre figures, but he is not using them to magnify their idiosyncracies. Similarly, when Stifter departs from probability and introduces fantastical and improbable events, his purpose is always to throw light on permanent and normal conditions: he uses fairy-stories but does not write them. There is a hidden wisdom and sanity in these stories, which becomes perceptible only when we have allowed all that is odd and peculiar in them to make its full impression. On the other hand, we may feel that his wisdom lacks that generality and universality which induces us to use such a word rather than 'a bundle of acute local observations'. That is to say, such wisdom as he has is limited by its close adhesion to the particular material (class, social and economic) that he works with. Stifter therefore was wise not to attempt to present man in all his fullness but to give young people such a prominent part in many of his stories; that is to say, some of his limitations make his strength. He is in *Bunte Steine* a good writer in a minor mode. While it would be unfair to Stifter to disregard the lessons he undoubtedly thought could be drawn from his stories, it would be fantastic to treat him as a guru, as he sometimes is. At his best he was an artist with a serious purpose.

Stifter strikes home through and in his style which is potent and gives his comparatively simple and not very original philosophy of life great persuasive power. It is not the much-admired purple passages, but the staple of his prose which marks him as a genuine artist. A bigger mind than the actual material of his stories would allow us to assume, emerges in the very way he writes. He uses many effects but it is the sum total which they form in the reader's mind when he has finished reading the tale which gives the style its potency. The shaped total of his stories marks the designing mind. Stifter leaves the raw material, the queer little tales he starts from, behind, but when he has finished with them they are worked on and worked up, 'durch-komponiert' as the Germans call it, 'finished' as Henry James says, who did the same with not very pointed anecdotes.

Talking of style in general has not very much meaning. A particular example is required to make the point of the preceding paragraph. In *Bergkristall* the description of the mountain which I mentioned in a previous chapter is the second of a total of six such descriptions in the story. This accumulation of descriptions of the same landscape or the same object or the same person is in itself an important and often-used stylistic feature in all the *Bunte Steine* stories. Stifter brings the point out by deliberate repetition with minor changes of a single theme as, for example, the forests in the changing light of the day in *Granit*, the various aspects of the Kar valley, the repeated descriptions of the priest himself in *Kalkstein*, the gilded angel guarding the girl's cradle in *Turmalin*, the path to the Nußberg in *Katzensilber* and many more. Stifter modifies them each time by subtle changes of viewpoint, by the use of varying epithets, the highlighting of different details, the play of light and shadow on them, or the telling traces of the passing of the seasons and years, yet all the time emphasising their essential sameness. We become attuned to these repetitions of motifs, to the monotony of descriptive detail, recurring phrases, significant sentences, and acknowledge their importance and start using them — as Stifter wants us to — as important pointers to the meaning of the story.

Although in the description of the mountain every detail helps to fill out and carry the story forward, by the introduction of the generalising word 'man' as the observer,

> Wenn man auf die Jahresgeschichte des Berges sieht, so sind im Winter die zwei Zacken seines Gipfels, die sie Hörner heißen, schneeweiß und stehen, wenn sie an hellen Tagen sichtbar sind, blendend in der finstern Bläue der Luft ... (p.143),

the mountain is made to speak directly to us and what it says so directly matters a lot more than what it meant for the villagers; or, if this seems an exaggeration, we could still say that what we are in contact with is a part of Stifter's mind, which he could not use for communication in any other way. For the most striking feature of the passage is that it does not make us dwell on its rhythmical force for its own sake. This larger meaning which we hear, we hear through the style. It is a means, not an end. We are sure here that Stifter is not trying to put across one of his moral intuitions. The mountain is not God or a symbol for moral awareness. We gain an intimation that here we are offered something finer, something closer to a reality he was apprehending immediately.

It is in such passages where the 'Dichter' predominates over the mere narrator that we cease to think of Stifter as confined either to the mid-nineteenth century or to a rather provincial backwater of Europe. Our whole difficulty, however, comes when we say he is speaking to us. He is not speaking to our everyday selves nor is he speaking of our everyday concerns. If I may put it extravagantly, the secretive is speaking to the secretive, but what passes between them is nearer to the frightening reality of nature and human nature than those comparatively vulgar explosions of storm and flood which are so often praised in Stifter's work. In fact I can sum up my whole claim for Stifter by saying that if he is at any point a permanent classic it is when, in Samuel Johnson's phrase, his wonderful prose awakens those ideas which lie slumbering in the heart of man.

There is, however, no doubt that his art was confined by having to flower in a world so hostile to all the author's values. The Stifter of *Bunte Steine* is a saddened man, who found it very bitter to have to observe that the evidence for the progressive improvement of mankind under the working of a moral law was rapidly diminishing with every subsequent development of the revolution that started in 1848. Political events only increased his inherent fears and darkened his hopes for the more generous impulses of humanity. The closing paragraphs of his *Vorrede* merely underline what he was forced to portray in his best stories. He was born to write of a movement upwards and was forced to portray a decline that he thought might well be permanent. Consequently, we may well suppose that we never have the whole of Stifter's mind in any one of these tales. Readers who are irritated when they find him secretive should turn to the pages of history, and not merely of the history of Austria, which show what solid reasons Stifter had for thinking that a glorious sun had set in his lifetime.

Chronological Table

1805 October 23. Stifter born at Oberplan (Southern Bohemia).

1818 Entered the Benedictine monastery school of Kremsmünster.

1826 Moved to Vienna to read law. Also studied mathematics and natural sciences. Earned his living as private tutor and landscape painter.

1827 Fell in love with Fanni Greipl but failed to marry her.

1837 Married to Amalia Mohaupt.

1844-1850 *Studien*, published in six volumes. All the thirteen stories (*Der Condor, Das Haidedorf, Feldblumen, Die Narrenburg, Die Mappe meines Urgroßvaters, Der Hochwald, Abdias, Brigitta, Das alte Siegel, Der Hagestolz, Der Waldsteig, Zwei Schwestern, Der beschriebene Tännling*) had previously appeared in earlier versions in magazines and almanachs.

1848 March Revolution in Vienna. Stifter moved to Linz. Articles on politics and educational matters.

1850 Appointed to the post of inspector of the primary and secondary schools in Upper Austria.

1853 *Bunte Steine*. Apart from *Katzensilber*, these stories also had first appeared in earlier versions from 1843 onwards.

1854 *Lesebuch zur Förderung humaner Bildung*. This anthology for older children was not accepted by the government for use in schools.

1856 Stifter deprived of the inspectorate of secondary schools.

1857 *Der Nachsommer*.

1865 *Nachkommenschaften*; *Witiko*, first volume.

1866 *Der Kuß von Sentze*; *Witiko*, second volume.

1867 *Witiko*, third volume; *Die Mappe meines*

Urgroßvaters, unfinished.

1867   December. Stifter fell ill with cirrhosis of the liver.

1868   January 28. Stifter died after a suicide attempt.

Select Bibliography

ABBREVIATIONS OF PERIODICALS

DVjS   Deutsche Vierteljahrsschrift für Literaturwissenschaft und
           Geistesgeschichte
Euph.   Euphorion
GR   Germanic Review
MLR   Modern Language Review
Neophil.   Neophilologus
VASILO Vierteljahrsschrift des Adalbert-Stifter-Instituts des Landes
           Oberösterreich
ZfdP   Zeitschrift für deutsche Philologie

A. EDITIONS OF STIFTER'S WORKS

Werke und Briefe. Historisch-kritische Gesamtausgabe, edited by Alfred
     Doppler and Wolfgang Frühwald (Stuttgart, Kohlhammer, 1978-).
     Vol.II/1 *Bunte Steine, Journalfassungen*, edited by Helmut Bergner
     (1982).
     Vol.II/2 *Bunte Steine, Buchfassungen*, edited by Helmut Bergner
     (1982).
Sämmtliche Werke, edited by August Sauer, Franz Hüller, Kamill Eben, Gustav
     Wilhelm, Klaus Zelewitz (Prag, Reichenberg, Graz, Hildesheim,
     1901-1979), 25 volumes.
*Bunte Steine, Erzählungen. Vollständige Ausgabe nach dem Wortlaut der
     Erstausgabe* (2 Bände, Pest und Leipzig, 1853), edited and with an
     afterword by Hannelore Schlaffer (München, Goldmann, 1983).

B. GENERAL AND CRITICAL STUDIES

1. Blackall, Eric, *Adalbert Stifter: A Critical Study* (Cambridge, University
    Press, 1948).
2. Naumann, Ursula, *Adalbert Stifter* (Stuttgart, Metzler, 1979).
3. Selge, Martin, *Adalbert Stifter: Poesie aus dem Geiste der Naturwissen-
    schaft* (Stuttgart, Kohlhammer, 1976).
4. Stern, J.P., *Re-Interpretations* (London, Thames and Hudson, 1964).
5. Tielke, Martin, *Sanftes Gesetz und Historische Notwendigkeit: Adalbert
    Stifter zwischen Restauration und Revolution* (Frankfurt, Bern, Peter
    Lang, 1979).
6. Swales, Martin and Erika, *Adalbert Stifter. A Critical Study*
    (Cambridge, University Press, 1984).

7. Wildbolz, Rudolf, *Adalbert Stifter. Langeweile und Faszination* (Stuttgart, Kohlhammer, 1976).

C. *CRITICAL STUDIES OF 'BUNTE STEINE'*

a) The collection as a whole

8. Bleckwenn, Helga, 'Adalbert Stifters *Bunte Steine*. Versuch zur Bestimmung der Stellung im Gesamtwerk', *VASILO* 21 (1972), pp.105-18.
9. Domandl, Sepp, 'Die philosophische Tradition von Adalbert Stifters "Sanftem Gesetz"', *VASILO*, 21 (1972), pp.79-103.
10. Klieneberger, H.R., 'The image of childhood in *Bunte Steine*', in *Adalbert Stifter heute: Londoner Symposium 1983*, edited by J. Lachinger, A Stillmark and M. Swales, (Linz, Adalbert-Stifter-Institut; London, Institute of Germanic Studies, 1985), pp.129-34.
11. Mason, Eve, 'Adalbert Stifters *Bunte Steine*: Versuch einer Bestandsaufnahme', ibid., pp.75-85.
12. Mühlher, Robert, 'Natur und Mensch in Stifters *Bunten Steinen*', *Dichtung und Volkstum (Euph.)*, 40 (1939), pp.295-304.
13. Requadt, Paul, 'Stifters *Bunte Steine* als Zeugnis der Revolution' in Stiehm, Lothar (ed.), *Adalbert Stifter: Studien und Interpretationen* (Heidelberg, Lothar Stiehm, 1968).
14. Stopp, Frederick, 'Die Symbolik in Stifters *Bunten Steinen*', *DVjS* 28 (1954), pp.165-93.
15. Thurnher, Eugen, 'Stifters "sanftes Gesetz"' in *Unterscheidung und Bewahrung: Festschrift H. Kunisch* (Berlin, De Gruyter, 1961).

b) Individual stories

Granit

16. Hahn, Walter, 'Zeitgerüst und Zeiterlebnis bei Stifter: *Granit*', *VASILO* 22 (1973), pp.9-16.
17. Ketelsen, Uwe K., 'Geschichtliches Bewußtsein als literarische Struktur. Zu Stifters Erzählung aus der Revolutionszeit *Granit* (1848/52)', *Euph.* 64 (1970), pp.306-25.
18. Swales, Martin, *The German Novelle* (Princeton, University Press, 1977), Ch.VII, 'Stifter: *Granit*'.

Kalkstein

19. Geulen, Hans, 'Stifterische Sonderlinge. *Kalkstein* und *Turmalin*. Eine Polemik', *Jahrbuch der Schiller-Gesellschaft* 17 (1973), pp.415-31.
20. Müller, Joachim, '*Die Pechbrenner* und *Kalkstein*: Strukturanalyse einer Urfassung und einer Endfassung der *Bunten Steine*', *VASILO* 15 (1966), pp.1-22.
21. Rath, Rainer, 'Zufall und Notwendigkeit. Bemerkungen zu den beiden Fassungen in Stifters Erzählung *Der arme Wohltäter* (I), *Kalkstein* (II)', *VASILO* 13 (1964), pp.70-80.

22. Reddick, John, 'Tiger und Tugend in Stifters *Kalkstein*. Eine Polemik', *ZfdP* 95 (1976), pp.235-55.
23. Ritter, Frederick, 'Der sanfte Mensch', *VASILO* 9 (1960), pp.72-78.

Turmalin
24. Hertling, G.H., '"Wer jetzt kein Haus hat, baut sich keines mehr". Zur Zentralsymbolik in Adalbert Stifters *Turmalin*', *VASILO* 26 (1977), pp.17-34.
25. Mason, Eve, 'Stifter's *Turmalin*. A Reconsideration', *MLR* 72 (1977), pp.348-58.
26. Müller, Joachim, 'Stifters *Turmalin*: Erzählhaltung und Motivstruktur. Ein Vergleich beider Fassungen', *VASILO* 17 (1968), pp.33-44.

Bergkristall
27. Küpper, Peter, 'Literatur und Langeweile. Zur Lektüre Stifters', in Stiehm, Lothar (ed.), *Adalbert Stifter* (see *13*), pp.171-88.
28. Schmidt, Hugo, 'Eishöhle und Steinhäuschen. Zur Weihnachtssymbolik in Stifters *Bergkristall*', *Monatshefte* (Wisconsin) 56 (1964), pp.321-35.
29. Schwarz, Egon, 'Zur Stilistik von Stifters *Bergkristall*', *Neoph.* 38 (1954), pp.260-68.
30. Whiton, John, 'Symbols of Social Renewal in Stifter's *Bergkristall*', *GR* 47 (1972), pp.259-80.

Katzensilber
31. Mason, Eve, 'Stifter's *Katzensilber* and the Fairy-Tale Mode', *MLR* 77 (1982), pp.114-29.
32. Müller, Joachim, 'Menschenwelt, Naturereignis, Symbolbezug und Farblichkeitsstruktur in Adalbert Stifters Erzählung *Katzensilber*', *VASILO* 31 (1982), pp.145-67.

Bergmilch
33. Himmel, Hellmuth, *Adalbert Stifters Novelle* Bergmilch. *Eine Analyse* (Köln und Wien, Böhlau, 1973).
34. Irmscher, Hans Dietrich, 'Adalbert Stifters Erzählung *Bergmilch*', *ZfdP* 88 (1969), pp.161-89.